The New Man in Christ

By
G. A. Studdert Kennedy

Edited by the Dean of Worcester

D0914697

Hodder and Stoughton
Limited   London
St. Paul's House
Warwick Square, E.C.4
mcmxxxii

First published	-	-	March, 1932
Reprinted	-	-	-	March, 1932
Reprinted	-	-	-	April, 1932
Reprinted	-	-	-	May, 1932

Made and Printed in Great Britain for Hodder and Stoughton Limited, by
Wyman and Sons Ltd., London, Reading and Fakenham

Preface

A FEW weeks before his death Arthur Hird wrote to tell
me that he had looked through a number of Studdert
Kennedy's unpublished MSS. and had selected some,
especially his notes for Retreat addresses, for publication.
Mr. Hird was of opinion that these addresses would
make a suitable book for Lenten reading, and be useful
to those who were preparing Lent addresses and sermons.
Before he could carry out his intention Arthur Hird was
stricken with illness and, exhausted by overwork as
editor and preacher, was unable to combat disease and
therefore passed away. His death is a loss to the cause
of the Christian faith in England.

Hird's unfinished work was sent to me with a request
that I would see it through the Press, a request I could
not refuse, as both Studdert Kennedy and Arthur Hird
were friends of mine.

Moreover, as I had, at Kennedy's request, seen his
first book, "The Hardest Part," through the Press, the
idea that I should do the same by his last strongly appealed
to me.

Some who are familiar with the bright, arresting, con-
versational style of Kennedy's books, such as "Lies,"
or "Fed Up" may think that these addresses are very
unlike Kennedy. It must be remembered, however,
that Studdert Kennedy was a popular orator accustomed
to express himself in such ways as would arrest the
attention of public meetings and express his meaning
in the way ordinary people would understand.

v

Preface

When writing his popular books he expressed himself in the manner which he found effective on the platform.

But the Retreat addresses here published were given to entirely different audiences—to small bodies of devout men and women of education, and in most cases largely composed of clergy—hence a difference in style so unlike that of the breezy, popular orator.

Moreover, these addresses were not written for publication and were not corrected by the author. They are in the nature of extensive notes. Had Studdert Kennedy revised these addresses for publication he would probably have recast some of them and have inserted some vivid illustrations.

All that I could legitimately do was to smooth out tangled sentences and correct obvious mistakes.

Except for such editorial corrections these addresses are preserved as Kennedy wrote them and therefore express the thoughts of a great spiritual prophet of our age.

The later portion of the book, however, does not consist of notes for addresses at Retreats, but of addresses which were left ready for publication. Here Kennedy may be seen at his best, thoughtful and deeply spiritual, and able in wonderful graphic way to link up the fundamental theology of the Christian Faith with the problems which confront us all in connection with modern life. No one can read unmoved the address on "Man shall not live by Bread alone," or that on "The Shepherd who maketh his sheep lie down in green pastures."

W. MOORE EDE.

Contents

The New Man in Christ

The New Life in Christ

Introduction

WE all have happy days or weeks that stand out in our memory, like jewels that we keep treasured up. A Retreat may be such a time, but it ought to be that and much more. It has little connection with the past, and no link with the future, but it ought not to leave us as we came ; those who come here ought when they leave to be changed beings. We say we are free to make a new beginning, but new beginnings are very hard, and our freedom is limited first by our heredity and then by our environment. But although it is limited it is nevertheless very real. There is part of me which is governed neither by heredity nor environment, and which can be changed and moulded by God. A sin is always a sin, and yet a sin repented of may turn into a real blessing to us. Thank God the sin is not us.

Let us this first evening be perfectly quiet and hold communion with God ; let us listen to His Voice, forget all about the world and its worries, and home worries, let us just be still and listen. No priest or teacher can do anything really for us, except to lead us to the door ; we have to knock ourselves, and we can only knock—*God only* can open, so we really can do nothing. How often have strong efforts only led to failure and tears : it is not we that can do anything by our efforts, it is only God that can turn us, and come to us, so let us be still and wait, only blessing Him and thinking of all His mercies to us.

Birth of the new life

The new life, that is what we want to find. New, does not involve a question of time, it is equivalent to Everlasting, Eternal. Age does not really exist; there are no old people in Heaven, there are only children.

What we really need is the new or Everlasting life, or in other words, Conversion. This new life may come suddenly, but normally it comes gradually. There is day and then there is night, but between them there is dawn, and no one knows when night ends and day begins, there is only gradually more light. This Retreat is to be a stage further for us, it is to bring us more new life; there is to be a break in the clouds, with a flood of light in our life; there is to be more " new life." All life responds to stimulus; we move when we are touched. The difference between only human and divine life, is the power to be touched by God, and so touched that all our life becomes " God centred " instead of being self-centred; that is the essence of the new life. We sometimes feel that the new life brings us so close to God that other things lose all their interest, and our intellectual abilities seem to decay.

The Gospels are a series of pictures, each presenting God in a different aspect; only they are put one after another and we look at them separately, but now we want to hang them up all together and view the whole gallery.

The first picture is that of the Holy Family—Christmas.

But first of all we must remember to associate the artist with the picture : it is not only a picture but the artist's self trying to press itself upon us, like a speaker by his words presses his spirit upon his hearers. God's love is the first thing that impresses us as we look at the Holy Family, His restless, resistless Love. He is always seeking us, using any means, going anywhere, not minding His dignity, in fact God has no dignity, so long as He can win a soul. He does not mind His message being bawled at the street corner, in fact He rather likes it, so long as the message is delivered and wins souls to Him.

Then the second picture is the power of weakness. He is weak as a child, He is mocked, spitted on, made a laughing stock, and yet His weakness is the greatest power. His great humility, His tenderness, are always there ; He never wants to punish us, our only punishment is being separated from Him. So we too shall be a power if we forget to assert ourselves, if we are meek, and gentle, and loving. The Power of His Love is Almighty, so if we speak of God Almighty, it is the same as if we said " God is Love." The power of His Love is shown in the Blessed Virgin, who although she did not understand rightly what had happened to her, yet entirely surrendered herself ; and that is what Jesus asks of us : complete self-surrender ; it is when we have entirely surrendered ourselves that the new life comes to us, and the Vision will get brighter and brighter and lead us to Him.

We should always remember that we are the Sons of God and the Inheritors of the Kingdom of Heaven.

Temptation

The next picture we have of Our Lord is that of His Temptation. Fewer pictures have been painted of the Temptation than of the Holy Family. One of the best is that by Dicksee which represents Our Lord quite alone, sitting down, with stones all round Him, in the grey light of dawn, with a face of intense suffering and deep thought He is concentrated on the thought how to do His Work, and He has come to the Wilderness so as to fight it out, to struggle with the thought of it. The real bodily presence of Satan, or Our Lord's body moving from one place to another is not probable, but the struggle and Temptation are just the same. He went to the Wilderness to be still, and He carried with Him His past, which we know only in small parts. He was quite conscious that He had a Call; already when He was twelve and was found in the Temple, doing His Father's business, He knew it.

His home as far as we know was not a happy one : He had an ideal Mother, but she did not understand Him, His brothers did not believe in Him. " These are my mother and my brethren." Home is the place where we undergo the best discipline, a discipline we can get nowhere else. Our Lord knew He had a call, He was conscious of that, but there was a great difference between what He knew He was, and what He really was.

We also have to go out into the wilderness and see what we are and what our call is. His was a specially severe struggle as He was sinless, and we none of us are. Temptation must not be mistaken for sin ; the purer we are the more temptations we shall have, but the more victorious we shall come out of them.

His Temptation took three forms :

(1) About the method of doing His work. The stones all round suggested bread and He was hungry, and His hunger at once made Him think of all the masses of people who were hungry, and whom He felt He could satisfy with His genius. That would have been the easier task, but He rejects it, as He is conscious that it is the lower, easier line, that men are still more in need of spiritual food. A mother can make everything easy and soft for her children, but teaching them to help themselves is far harder and much better. The only way to help anybody is by turning our minds from our happiness to doing the Will of God.

(2) The second temptation was that of founding a Kingdom on earth, but He rejects it on the same ground, because it is no use dealing with the outside until we have dealt with the inner man.

(3) The third temptation is to pursue the methods of the world, but nothing will succeed except spiritual reformation, and a spirit of faith.

These Temptations teach us :

1st. That we have to meet our temptations in a spirit of faith in God and in our better selves. Most of our temptations come from our work. We should not be concerned mainly with our spiritual peace and happiness. We have become much too introverted, instead of being extraverted, and our prayers are always I, I, I, and in that way we manufacture temptation. In the same way in Self-Examination and Confession we should not dwell too much on small details, but examine ourselves on broader lines, dealing with our work and our relations with other people.

2nd. That no work is of any value unless it is done in a sacramental way. The world is very poor in spiritual power, and although work is necessary, like giving the cup of water to the thirsty, yet we cannot do anything of ourselves, but if we work and give ourselves as the sons of God, then our work is of infinite value and we may do much for others.

3rd. For their sakes, the others, we must consecrate ourselves and in consequence we must surrender ourselves entirely, but it is all for *their* sakes. If you seek peace and happiness you will not find them; you will only secure them as far as you seek them in Service.

We are in danger of becoming purely devotional, making devotions an end in themselves instead of a means of reaching Him and doing our work for Him. There is the leaven of devotional people in the world, but they do not leaven the lump, the world, because they do not consecrate their devotions to God and His Service, that is the only way : Consecration of our work.

Transfiguration

Devotion on the Mount.

Service in the plain.

Let us think of Fra Angelico, or even better of Raphael's pictures. See how the Transfiguration happens : " As he was praying," that was His wont, His ordinary practice, and He saw His new mission, and then He found Himself up against His past, and felt all its limitations. Even His disciples felt the force of tradition and were limited by it, and it must have been a sore trial to Our Lord as He lived so close with them. So when Our Lord asks Peter and receives the answer full of joy, " Thou art the Christ," it brought forth praise for Peter, but even then a sadness to Jesus, as He knew His weakness. So He went up a mountain to pray ; there is something soothing in going up, it lifts one above the plain, and the every-day life, and brings one in a larger atmosphere, and enlarges our Vision. We know what kind of prayer Our Lord would use, as He has left us a model, the Lord's Prayer. Notice how the first three petitions are *Thy* name, *Thy* Kingdom, *Thy* will, and then only *Our* bread, *Our* sins, *Our* temptations (not my), and then He switches back to God's Glory. And that Glory leads to the Transfiguration, as it brings God's Glory to this earth.

The Lord's Prayer is the essence of prayer, it makes us realise that we are part of the brotherhood, and that we are not to hold Communion simply as single individuals with our Father, not even when we pray by our bedside, all by ourselves, we must still remember others. When Jesus went up the mountain He was feeling His load was too heavy for Him to bear, so He lifts it up to God and He won to the very Height of God, and makes Him the centre and He Himself becomes one with the whole vast world scheme, and His answer is so complete that when He descends the answer to prayer shines in His eyes, and Peter being heavy with sleep sees Him transfigured.

The Transfiguration is the symbol of Answered Prayer. It is a perfect prayer, perfectly answered, not by lifting the difficulty and pain, but by making Him one with the whole scheme, making Him one with God. So it is with us. Bring the world up into the mountain with us and pray, and lay it all before God, determined not to be dragged down by anything. The world would say continually : " You can't, you can't do it," and the stars cry out, " You can, you can." Even if we have only a small job to do, and it is done in a large way, it becomes a big thing, and it makes it fit in harmoniously with the world scheme.

But you have to come down from the mountain, and

you will find people crying out for help. "Lord, come to my son," and that is well depicted in Raphael's picture. But come down in body, not in mind, keep your heart on the heights. God calls out to you that His yoke is easy, because it is harmonious with the rest of the scheme, just as by fitting the yoke of an ox you can lighten his load.

We also have our mountain of Transfiguration, let us pray that this Retreat may be one ; our Sacraments ought to be. The Mass is such a big, tremendous thing, and we so often make it a little thing by forgetting to think of worship, and that we worship with Angels and Archangels ; the Bread which ought to represent all necessary things, only represents bread, the Wine which ought to remind us of all beauty, is only wine, and so we miss much of the true worship, and our prayers are only little things.

Gethsemane

This is by far the most awful picture, and it seems as if we could hardly look at it without irreverence. And indeed, we could not look at it at all unless it were that behind Gethsemane is Easter and the empty tomb. Reverence in looking at this picture will consist in thinking of it clearly. It tells us of two things :

1. What sin means to God.
2. What it ought to mean to sons of God.

But first of all it does not tell us about the origin of sin, that is an insoluble problem. Many books have been written about it, but they leave it just as insoluble ; it appears in the Garden of Eden, but how ? Some say it was brought by fallen Angels. But who brought it to the Angels ?

Evil is irrational and unreasonable. What Christ

came to teach us is not the explanation of evil, but that
He came to destroy it, and we ought to do the same.

He first teaches us about the seriousness of sin
(which is a mild way of putting it). Some people just
ignore sin, but that is not Christ's way ; it is easy at
the beginning, but there comes a time when it will not
be possible. You can ignore the sin of the man who
ruins another man's daughter, but what about the man
who ruins your daughter ? We must set ourselves
against ignoring sin.

Some of our friends, and earnest friends, to fight evil
concentrate on two main lines :

(1) Education.
(2) Improvement of environment.

Both are excellent in their way, but quite ineffective
in their results. Education coupled with evil makes
clever devils. Environment can be purified up to a
certain point, but men drag down their environment
to their own level.

The objection of the world to dealing with sin is
that it sets up a conflict in us, and the conflict can be so
terrible that it sets up nervous diseases, and it has
devastating effects caused by the effort needed for the
struggle. None but a Priest who hears Confessions,
and the nerve specialist, know the effect of the conflict
in man's soul. Many a mill girl has turned from
religion as she said she felt happier without it, and so
she does at the beginning, but that happiness does not
last. It is no good trying to stifle the struggle, it does
not die, it only goes on subconsciously. Worrying
about sin is a great danger to religious people ; it turns
people from Christianity. But Christ came to save us
from worrying about sin.

Gethsemane and Christianity have added to the
struggle, as people try to explain how Christ who was

sinless should have to suffer, and why had He to undergo His agony. It was explained by the idea of Sacrifice. Some said sacrifice to a righteous God ; others, sacrifice to the devil, or to a number of other things. But one thing was lost sight of and that is that nothing, even sin, can alienate us from the love of God, and Christ came to bring us that revelation. Even if we spit in Christ's face, He still goes on saying " I love you, I love you, I still love you." It is not God that needs to be reconciled to men, it is men that need reconciliation with God.

When we read : " And the Lord laid upon him the iniquity of us all," who is the Lord ? We know that the Lord is Love. So it is " Love that lays upon him the iniquity," and that explains much better what it means. If your son disgraced you, you would feel and bear the disgrace just as much as he does ; and then when the load becomes too heavy you say you cannot bear it alone, God must help you and He answers from the Cross : " I have, I do. Your sins are my sins, your disgrace is my disgrace, and I am not broken by it, I live for ever."

We should not only bear our sins, we should help Christ to bear the sins of the world ; we should be sin bearers. It is an intolerable burden and it cannot be borne without God.

There is an easy, amiable way of looking at sin, like the motto that hangs sometimes in bedrooms :

> " There is so much good in the worst of us
> And so much bad in the best of us
> That it does not behove any of us
> To be hard on the rest of us."

Another way of looking at it is the pharisaism which judges others, so as not to have to judge ourselves.

Christ laid upon us the necessity of the conflict (1) for our sins, (2) for the world's sins.   And the world has need of sin bearers.

Calvary

Sin is a knot that it takes God to unravel.   What is the knot that is to be untied ?

(1) It is the *sin of the past*.   For a long time the legend of our names being written in a book was current, and in all the apocalyptic writings that imagery is used. Modern science—Psychology—has now shown us what the book is on which all our acts, and words and thoughts are written ;   it has revealed to us that there is no such thing as forgetting, but that everything is written in the subconscious self and there remains for ever.

(2) *The Guilt of the Past*.   Past sin operates now, and cripples our activity ;   shame of our sin takes away the harmony of our lives.   The self that has committed a sin and is not forgiven has to live with our higher self.   The reconciling of the two selves by God is the only way to spiritual harmony.

The Consequence of sin.   That cannot be stopped.   We can be forgiven ourselves, but the consequence of our sin goes in ever widening circles, and nothing can stop that.

(3) *The Fear of the Future*.   We have to reckon with the strength of habit.   There are times, as in this Retreat, when it seems impossible we should ever do wrong, commit sin, that is when we are at our best ;   but habit has a physical basis, it ploughs a furrow in our constitution and we return to our sin.   That is the knot we have to untie.   The efforts to untie it without God's help have been very numerous, but none have met with success.   The untying of the knot has always for Christians gathered round the Cross of Christ.   In " The

Pilgrim's Progress " when Christian sees the Cross on the Hill, his burden falls from him down the abyss. The constant experience of Christians is that they obtain release through the Cross of Christ.

There are two sides to the power of the Cross; Theology and Experience. The theology of the Cross is not a peculiarly helpful study; we must however differentiate between the theology of the Cross and the release or deliverance effected by the Cross, which unties the knot of sin.

The first word on the Cross to the penitent thief gives us the first and best clue to God's attitude to sin; it must be taken in all simplicity; it is spoken by God through man, and tells us that the Father is loving, that sin does not alientate God from the sinner. God loves you whatever you are or do; He has no dignity; there is nothing He will not stoop to; He loves you, He knows you, He wants you, He can make something of you, if only you come to Him. God knows you better than you know yourself. He knows the ugliness of sin and loathes it, but He is eternally loving to the sinner. Forgiveness, if you realise it, comes to you as a thrill of sudden surprise, it takes hold of you, only you must believe you are forgiven and not doubt. The Cross reveals the hideousness of sin, but it also reveals the victory over sin by Christ, the intense and resistless and eternal love of God.

The danger is that some of us cannot think of Christ because of the Cross, and yet His Majesty, and the Majesty of the mind of Christ is what should attract us and is what is saving us. The Cross is God's language, and He speaks to us in it in human terms.

(1) It calls us to stop to think. That is always the beginning : we have to stop. To many who pass by it is nothing at all. The Cross called to the thief and

made him stop and think, and then his heart was turned.

(2) The Cross calls us to self-examination and Confession. It is the turning to Jesus. Confession of our sins is always the first step to Conversion. Private Confession does not always succeed with all people. In the region of Psychology it produced Psycho-analysis, with its many dangers. It often turns the attention from Christ to the Cross. That is what the danger of detailed Confession is ; it tempts you to think more of sin than of God, and that is what must be avoided. It is that on which your attention is most constantly fixed, that reproduces itself most. It is the knowledge of the love of God, whatever our sins may be, that saves us ; so come to Confession with your mind fixed on Absolution.

Beauty and goodness and truth all are one in God.

Crucifixion

The first effect of the Cross on the thief was to stop and make him think, and then he made his confession, in which he speaks of the Kingdom of Christ ; he does not know what the kingdom is but he recognises Kingship in the figure hanging on the Cross by him, and he has begun to adore something that is beautiful and good and true because they are beautiful and good and true, and to love Jesus because He is Jesus. And his confession is received at once with generous welcome, he only asked to be remembered, but he was told that He will be in Paradise ; and Jesus' answer begins with the emphatic words " Verily, Verily." That is the eternal and everlasting road of forgiveness. There are two parts in it that we must untie ourselves, confession and faith to believe it. The Christian says that there is no other road by which the knot can be untied, and the world by psycho-analysis, reaffirms it. Psycho-analysis shows us the method by which the mind works ; it claims that to get rid of what harms you, you must bring the thought from the subconscious self to the surface and to bring it to the light of day. It also tells us that the more you *will* a thing, the more you find yourself unable to do it. As St Paul says, " The good that I would that I do not, and the evil that I would not, that I do."

But thanks be to God who gives us the victory through Jesus Christ Our Lord. It is the imagination that helps us most. We really realise the things we imagine and picture. We are touched by poverty at our very doors, but when we hear of an earthquake at San Francisco, we let it pass over our mind and are not touched by it. Christians assert that it is not what you will, but what you worship that rules our life. The legend that St. Francis had the mark of the nails on his hands may most likely be true.

Christianity asserts that the Holy Spirit sanctifies the whole man, and cleanses the unconscious as well as the conscious self. Coué, with the Nancy school, asserts that you can dissolve a complex by pouring in its place what is good and true and beautiful, and that cleanses the subconscious mind, without having to bring to the surface all the ugly things stored in the subconscious mind, and that theory is upheld by the old Saints, and is much more healthy than psycho-analysis. By continual Communion with God we may become cleansed and entirely cured. That is forgiveness ; it destroys the power of sin, and transforms the guilt of sin into greater love for Our Lord Who loves us and therefore forgives us. Can we forgive ourselves ? No, not entirely, but we go on with greater love, and we try to pass on His love to His creatures.

The New Life in Christ

Easter

Now we pass from the sad mysteries of sin and shame and suffering to the Joy of Easter. And we must remember that it is by Joy that we are saved eventually, for joy passes into the power-house of our life.

When we think of sin in the future we are afraid, we fear that we may not be able to keep up what we have now risen to. The means whereby we are justified is through the Mystery of pain on the Cross, but the means whereby we are saved is the contemplation of the joys of God. This is what we need most here; it is the belief that we shall be able to keep on as we feel now. But when we look at the Cross we feel that it contains all the brutality and filth and dirt man is capable of, but Christ by His Majesty and Love has turned the pitch into gold, the dirt into purity. *He* has made Good Friday good.

The Cross has always been a banner of triumph. Joy has always been the characteristic of Christianity. The miracle of the Resurrection has been to many Christians both a triumph and a power of salvation. One could trace in poetry, rude and rough, all the history of the triumph of the Resurrection; and although the history of the Christian Church fills one with shame and dismay, we must remember that only the history of prominent people and striking movements is written, but that the real history of the Christian Church is written in Christian homes.

Now whence does this note of triumph come from? Apparently on Good Friday the world had triumphed, not Christ, and yet these men, His disciples, became a band of missionaries with a triumphant message, a message of new life.

There are two lines of evidence for the truth of

the Resurrection, one the evidence of the world, the other the Gospel narrative. The historians cannot help noticing the growth of Christianity, but they are at a loss to explain it, as the mystery seems insoluble to them ; still they note it, there is the evidence in the events in the world.

The Gospel narratives have passed through such awful criticism in the last eighty years as has never been undergone by any other writings, and on the whole they have come out unscathed.

Of course there are some people who do not believe in the Resurrection, because they disbelieve in any miracles ; it only shows they think they know everything about the Universe, or they would see that miracles are possible when there is an adequate cause for them. The world has not become less mysterious but more mysterious : they have lost the power of wonder and worship, and so they deny the Resurrection.

Our Salvation lies in the constant contemplation of the Resurrection. We know that our Redeemer lives because we can hold Communion with Him, and that is the truest evidence. Continually let us turn our mind to Christ triumphant. If we look at life in the light of the Resurrection, we shall grow in grace. As we grow in grace sin becomes more of an unreality, the reality is what we dwell on, and that ought to be the triumph of God. On Good Friday the Cross seemed the end; after Easter the Cross was never seen except through the Resurrection.

The perpetuation of forgiveness is sanctified by Easter Day, and our minds always dwelling on it, the conviction grows on us that we are forgiven and that death does not matter. Resurrection is the victory over sin and over death. The Resurrection fits life exactly with the Cross behind and the empty tomb, and we feel that death does not matter.

Ascension

The picture of the Ascension is painted for us in brief words in S. Luke's Gospel, " He ascended into Heaven." S. Luke's is the only Gospel which paints the picture for us, the other Evangelists only mention the fact. What moves us about the picture is its truth, and of course all beauty is true, as beauty *is* truth. There is no picture one can say one's prayer before, except the Crucifixion, that is more helpful. But many questions are hurled at it : Did He ascend ? Where is Heaven ? What is Heaven ? Was there really that May morning when He was parted from His disciples ? Did He ? And if He did, what difference does it make to me ? What help can I get from it ?

The question arises whether Our Lord did really ascend, or if the whole account is symbolical ? Anyhow, His sitting at the Right Hand of God can only be symbolical. Yet although we have only S. Luke's word for it, he is backed by the whole Christian consciousness. The Christians have always believed that Christ is now with God, His equal, reigning with Him in all His Majesty and Glory. It may have been clothed in a pictorial, traditional manner, but the essence of the picture is true, and if true why should He not have been lifted up as S. Luke describes. In any case it does not matter, it is true and fits in perfectly and we feel at peace before it, and it is full of teaching. Then about Heaven. Where is Heaven ? For men to be in heaven is to be with Jesus, and Jesus is Heaven. Heaven is a hand's breadth from a lily and is the meaning of the lily. So when we are told to set our affections on things above it means, set your affection on the meaning of things, and Jesus has come to mean for us that which gives meaning to the world. He sums up all the world, and that is Heaven. Jesus in that way passes from one particular to the universal. He is everywhere, in everything. He who was the Carpenter of Nazareth has stamped Himself on consciousness as the meaning of everything.

The Ascension is the climax and explanation of all the pictures we have been looking at, the Nativity, Transfiguration, Temptation, etc., it sums them all up in one picture. Life becomes filled with meaning when we look at it in the light of the Ascension. It is for us what the theory of Evolution is for the world, but even science has begun to find out that they explained man in the wrong way, going back to the animals from which we spring and forgetting the angels and archangels, with whom we have kinship, and Christ the perfect Man. We are in Him, and He is in us, striving upwards, giving meaning to our life, which otherwise seems such a jumble and loses its meaning. It brings us the Christ life, the new life, which we cannot see distinctly yet, but through a glass, darkly. When all our gifts are His gifts, our hands His hands, our tongue His tongue, then will the Kingdom of Heaven come on earth. If we had bravely contended that Evolution came from above we should have escaped many troubles. As Geddes says : " It is love and not struggle that is the world's law." We should look onward, not backward.

When we look on all the misery and pain and trouble in the city, we can see Christ crucified, but when we see people leaving their homes and comfort, surrendering themselves entirely to God and His work, then we see the Ascension and we are comforted and can bear the misery.

The New Life in Christ

IT IS NOT FINISHED

It is not finished, Lord.
There is not one thing done,
There is no battle of my life,
That I have really won.
And now I come to tell Thee
How I fought to fail,
My human, all too human, tale
Of weakness and futility.
And yet there is a faith in me,
That Thou wilt find in it
One word that Thou canst take
And make
The centre of a sentence
In Thy book of poetry.
I cannot read the writing of the years,
My eyes are full of tears,
It gets all blurred, and won't make sense
It's full of contradictions
Like the scribblings of a child,
But wild, wild
Hopes, and longing as intense
As pain, which trivial deeds
Make folly of—or worse :
I can but hand it in, and hope
That Thy great mind, which reads
The writings of so many lives,
Will understand this scrawl
And what it strives
To say—but leaves unsaid.
I cannot write it over,
The stars are coming out,
My body needs its bed.
I have no strength for more,
So it must stand or fall—Dear Lord—
    That's all.

agreeing on essentials. The only essentials are the Spiritual Gifts, and character.

Means of the Spirit

God works in His Church by means of the seven Sacraments, and most particularly the two special Sacraments. We are to carry them on as consistently as we can, but we must never let them become mere observances ; their effectiveness depends so much on our taking them with the full measure of the Incarnation behind them. Our Churchmanship ought to be the first thing in our life ; confession and absolution the means by which we are restored to full Membership.

Although we may come to our Communion in a little country Church with only half a dozen yokels with us, let us remember that in God's sight all the different Churches do not exist, for Him there is only *One* Altar, with *One* Priest and thousands of Communicants offering themselves to Him, and coming to worship Him. Come to the Sacrament recognising the whole teaching of the Incarnation. See in the Bread everything God has given us for our necessary use, and in the Wine all the beauty of the world. We so often fail because our Communion is a personal matter between us and God, and we miss communion with our neighbour Mrs. Jones. The Communion ought to become a great big thing, and we should see the whole world in the Sacrament. To begin with there is no common bread and wine, they are a wonder in themselves.

The Sacrament becomes a channel through which He urges Himself upon us, making bread and wine the means of vehicle of Himself. It is the work of the Spirit to make all things new, and to make us lead the new life. It is out of reverence for God that the courtesy for men is born.

The New Life in Christ

AT THE EUCHARIST

How through this Sacrament of simple things
The great God burns His way,
I know not—He is there.
The silent air
Is pulsing with the presence of His grace,
Almost I feel a face
Bend o'er me as I kneel,
While on my ears there steal
The strains of " Agnus Dei " softly sung.
How it calls—calls Heaven to earth,
Calls Christ to birth,
And pleads for man's Redemption
By his God.
Here star and sod
Unite to sing their Maker's praise,
While, through the windows, broken rays
Of crimson sunlight make a path
For Him to tread.
Just common bread ?
The artist's colour blazing bright,
The subtle scheme of shade and light,
That thrills our souls with ecstasy,
Is bread.
The notes that wed,
And weave a wonderland of sound,
Wherein our hearts may wander round,
And reach the heart of God's red rose,
Where beauty dwells alone and grows
Sublime in solitude,
All these are bread.
Are they not born of earth and rain
Becoming tissue of man's brain,
The vehicle of every thought ?
The Spirit that our God bestows,
The mystery that loves and knows,
The very soul our Saviour bought
Speaks through a body born of bread—

And wine.
The clinging vine
That climbs some crumbled wall in France,
Drinks in the Love of God,
His precious Blood,
Poured out in beams that dance
Through long-drawn summer days,
Swift golden rays of sunshine,
That are stored within the grape
Until it swells
And spills their splendour
Into wine
To fill the chalice of the Lord.
Then earth and heaven intertwine;
The Word
Takes flesh and dwells with men,
And once again
Dim eyes may see
His gentle glory shine,
The glory of humility,
Which in creation stoops to raise,
Through time's eternity of days,
Our weakness to His strength,
For neither length,
Nor breadth nor depth nor height,
Stays now the piercing of that light
Of omnipresent Love,
It runs red fire through our veins;
That Life divine,
In common wine,
Thrills through the matter of our brains,
Begetting dreams,
And gleams
Of God—swift golden speech,
And charity that burns to reach
The very depths of hell,
And lift them up to Christ,
Who has our thirsty souls sufficed,
Till they are drunk with God.

The Beatitudes

In this Retreat we propose to consider the Beatitudes and trace their spiritual connection in the Sermon on the Mount. We find the Beatitudes give us a picture, a portrait, and it is the portrait of a King, the portrait of Jesus Christ our Lord, Jesus Who not only knows the Truth, but is the Truth.

First of all, however, let us consider the object of a Retreat under these three points : the Necessity, the Dangers, and the Responsibility of a Retreat.

We find that for all who work and for all in general, but especially for those who have to give out of their best and hardest, not only are periodical retreats necessary, but retreat hours in their life are absolutely essential. A preacher, especially one who lives his life in the presence of a crowd, who goes from one crowd to another is in great danger of dishonesty. The crowds cannot be ignored, and he tries to find out the truth not only for the truth's sake but for the sake of saying it to others.

He addresses a crowd when he addresses one sufferer, and he addresses one sufferer when he addresses a crowd. The world's atmosphere is for ever pressing on us, and we are in danger of becoming only a reflection of our world, our tiny world, instead of being ourselves, and expressing ourselves. The vast majority of people are only passengers, and their dead weight has to be lifted and moved, and the dangers are terrific.

Like children they are tossed to and fro, from one doctrine to another, always going crazy on a new doctrine.

The New Man in Christ

We are told by Aristotle that man is a social animal. That is not really true, man is a gregarious animal, who rather than live alone will live even with people whom he dislikes, and tears to pieces in his talk. The village life is clear proof of this. Every priest at some time has grieved because his people have come to the same Altar having feuds and enmities. It is only a question of appearance, as in any herd, the grey wolf will be at war with the white wolf. A Priest will not be hated for what he teaches, but he will be hated for wearing a Chasuble at Mass. Our sins, our lack of charity, envy, selfishness, put us on the level of animals. It is not only the common coarse people that are bestial, but one can see that bestial look of animosity even in refined old ladies.

Jesus based His hope of progress on the development of the individual. An individual is an end in itself, his contribution to life must not be a reflection, but a unique contribution, his own, and no one else's. There is always something unique in a leader, he is a personality. The same thing applies to everyone, and the poverty of personality is at present the greatest hindrance.

One object of this Retreat is to develop our personality. Our Lord taught as One having authority; it is this quality, in an infinitely lesser degree, that we must cultivate. The great feud between the Catholics and the Protestants is that the former bow to authority, and the latter maintain that you must judge by your personal conscience : the Christian of the future must combine both these doctrines. A rose in its marvellous beauty is the result of the whole universe and world, but each rose is unique and cannot be repeated. We also are unique, each different from the other. A Retreat is a place where you can be alone, and yet not alone, where you are endeavouring to be alone *with* God, but apart from others ; we are relieved from conversation which really does not help anybody, so we can be still and commune with God. We are not only miserable sinners, but we are also the children of God, and that is really us. We may narrow ourselves down to nothing but ourselves, but we ought to bring the world and all its suffering and need into our Retreat—the near East, Ireland, the unemployed, the sufferers of Russia, Austria, etc. So we shall be alone with God and the world. We want to sanctify ourselves for their sakes, we rise on the heights of prayer to get the help so as to go down into the plain to give the others what we have received, and live a life of Service.

Then as to the responsibility of a Retreat.

The first is what we have just mentioned. For their sakes we sanctify ourselves.

The second is that we may enlarge our individuality and personality, that we may become a distinct individual, not to separate ourselves from the world, but that we may get nearer to it and bear the burden of its sin.

A caution is necessary. We are not to worry, or to strain after a new experience, we are to take our world, the larger world, and bring it into the Presence of God in perfect and complete trust.

First Beatitude

"Blessed are the poor in spirit for theirs is the Kingdom of God."

The Sermon on the Mount is not only the law for the individual, it is also the law for the Kingdom, for the beloved community. It is not the law for the individual as against the beloved community, it is the law of the individual as fulfilled in the Community. It is an untrue conception of freedom to set the individual against the community. Intense individualism has been the curse of the nineteenth century. It is not Christ's teaching. Jesus always taught that the individual does not exist outside the community, nor the community without the individual. Such also is the relation of the Christian to the Church. Jesus was always conscious that He belonged to the world ; we are not only to be human, but humane in the widest sense of the world. If a great poet or artist sees the beauty of nature either he sings in his heart a song that makes other people see it, or the painter reproduces it in colours that make others see the beauty of it.

A mother brings up her child as if that child may turn some day into a great prophet or genius.

Someone said that good deeds that are done without the grace of God have a seed of evil in them, and it is true in a certain sense. We can only come into our Kingdom as we are part of the whole.

The idea of poverty and riches is the all-prevailing topic at present, it is a real obsession, and more books are written about it than about any other subject, and those books are more read than any other books ; it is nearly a disease. The text oft quoted, " The love of money is the root of all evil," is very true. The love of money does not only destroy the heart, but it destroys the intellect as well.

In every class however there is a remnant who rebel with pain against that love of money, and it is on them that the future rests. They rebel, it is true, but they cannot escape entirely ; they are forced to take notice of figures and computations as those figures represent human souls and bodies ; those human bodies do not suffer only poverty of body, but damnation of their souls. As the 51st Psalm says truly, our blood guiltiness is very true and real and we are responsible in great part.

Charity has become an evil word because people have been giving money but they have not given themselves. What the economic remedy is for all the poverty is difficult to say, as every remedy is dangerous, but the one surrounded with least danger consists in our taking up a family, helping them with money if necessary, but especially helping them like brothers and so stretching out hands of healing to them.

Jesus cut Himself free from all ties ; He was not married, His Mother was not dependent on Him ; He was no puritan, He took His share in the world's life. Piety and religion which consist in running away make one sick, they are a kind of funk holes.

All this may be thought not to be spiritual but worldly but it is essentially spiritual, as there is no spirituality which is not sacramental, and all life has to be sanctified and made sacramental. " Blessed are the poor in spirit." The essence of poverty is dependence, the poor accepts all, and in gratitude strives to give back all he can, but feels he still owes a debt he cannot pay. Jesus teaches we are all poor as we are in utter, complete dependence on God. All the unrest in the world comes from the burning effort to be free, not to be free in the beloved community, as part of it, but outside it. This is a lie which has brought after it murder, bloodshed, etc. There are two sides to that lie : domination and rebellion ; and those two make a vicious circle. We are all dependent on one another, only among the richer people the dependence is disguised. When we receive a dividend or share notice, that share is human beings. Poverty of spirit would really transform our plutocracy. The Kingdom of God can only be built by the poor in spirit ; there is a crying need for " poor in spirit " people, for those who make entire surrender of themselves, for those who will not rebel against the love of God, who resign all claim to independence and acknowledge all they owe to God, and the need of sacrificial giving.

The other way is to help by prayer, to pray with intelligence, to be clamorous for reform, reforms asked for by the rich are more likely to come true than those asked for by the poor themselves.

Jesus was not content to be God only, but became Incarnate; the spirituality that is worth anything is an Incarnation. It does not make the devotional life less necessary, but it makes it more necessary. It is the *Bread* that binds us all together. We must consecrate the ordinary things of life by the Sacraments; we must be bound by the Unity of Spirit. By the Sacrifice of the Mass we obtain Communion with God, but do we obtain communion with Mrs. Jones our neighbour? The poor in spirit go through life with thanks on their lips for all the beautiful, all the good.

Second Beatitude

" Blessed are they that mourn for they shall be comforted."

1. *Sin.* There is a modern cult of cheerfulness, and cheerfulness is prized almost higher than charitableness. It is partly good in the sense that it implies courage, but partly bad as it implies fear. Jesus was not a man of many tears; only twice it is recorded that He shed them, and then only for others, not for Himself, whereas we shed them mostly for ourselves. Emotion is not to be trusted, and sentimentality is a deadly enemy of religion. There is a great need to avoid excess of sentimentality, and yet there is no honest thought that does not feel, and feeling cannot be separated from the soul. Jesus could feel intense joy, could weep with sorrow, His eyes could flash with anger. We have only

just found out that scientific truth is only *part* truth. A chemist could analyse the Sistine Madonna, but although all its chemical components would be there, that could not explain its beauty and the effect of that beauty on others. We cannot exclude emotion, but we can blend it with the other parts.

The secret of wisdom is consecrated thought which goes on praying all the time, not only at stated times. Being poor in spirit adds to the burdens of your life, you are confronted with sorrow, there is no possibility of getting away from *sorrow, sin, ugliness,* you cannot shut your eyes to it, so you live in the shadow of death. This beatitude and the whole of them might be turned into " Blessed are the honest," which sums them up. We live in a fool's paradise, and we are so constituted that when one castle in the air is shattered we build another one, and so on, although castles in the air do not help us at all. What helps us is candour, courage, honesty ; we must face up to our sins. Some people think it is morbid to think of your sins, but far from it, as we want to bring back the sense of sin to the world as it is so prevalently lacking at present. Some think of God as of one who never overlooks a slight, whose dignity must not be offended, a kind of glorified policeman. Men always thinking of God in that light turned to Jesus to find the love they craved for, but Jesus came to reveal to us the nature of God, and showed us that He and God are the same, perfect Love. God has no dignity, is not concerned about it, therefore He has the most wonderful unfailing dignity. What He is concerned with is that the people who mock Him and cannot be won over will be damned. A person who is not concerned with his sins is so much dead weight that Love has to lift, as out of those persons the brotherhood of man cannot be built, and God is most concerned with that brotherhood, and He is more concerned with His Work than with Himself. Sin is never a private matter, it is always public, and is a sin against the brotherhood.

Through Confession we are restored to the brotherhood, and formerly one had to confess one's sins openly to the brotherhood assembled. The thing we must do is to fall in love with the beloved community, then you will feel and realise your sin as you never have before. Let us face our sins and then we will mourn for them, and that leads to comfort, as confession and penitence lead to absolution and forgiveness. Let us ask ourselves can a beloved community be built out of such as we are ? Face up to your sins and the sins of others with courage, and realise that other people's sins are partly your sins. If we love others we suffer for their sins, like a mother would feel a son's sin ; the only saints there are, are sin-bearers. The absence of sin-bearing in Christians is the most deep bedded sin, and goes to make the worst Pharisee, but it does not prove an escape. We try to escape by many gates—first by the gate of condemnation ; condemning others fiercely to absolve ourselves ; secondly, the gate of indifference ; we think their sins are no concern of ours. The real thing is that we are afraid ; it hurts to feel sin so we try to escape the pain. We run away through a back door from the Garden of Gethsemane : we are sheer cowards. Let us pray that we do not escape.

2. *Sorrow*. We have to stiffen our upper lip and be brave, strengthen our heart and say I will not give way. Other people's sorrows are hardest to bear, but we must mourn with them and they will be comforted. We find that much of what makes it hard to bear comes from our wrong idea of God. If we have thought that God is perfectly just and impartial and metes out sorrow

according as we deserve it, we shall certainly be disappointed. God has never promised that we shall have no pain and no sorrow. Good people suffer as much, if not more, than others. Jesus, the best Man, did. God gives not as we deserve but as much as we can receive. God is the Good Shepherd always seeking, battering at our doors. Shall we deny the sunshine because there are clouds ? Shall we deny the love of God because we have to suffer ? God does not *will* we should have to bear pain, but the Comfort is a call to courage. The mystery of evil is insoluble : it is there, why, whence ? We do not know and cannot explain it. The temptation is to turn bitter and despair. Sorrow in itself cannot do us any harm, if it does not break us ; conquer it and there will come a time when we shall look back upon that pain and sorrow and feel that it has only tried us but has passed over without harming us. As St. Paul said, " I believe that the sorrow of this world is nothing to be compared with the glory that shall be revealed to us." We are saved not by the Cross but by the Christ on the Cross. We sometimes go wrong trying to comfort the poor ; we must call upon their courage too. There is a joy in the very heart of pain, and we can only enjoy that joy when we have suffered pain.

3. *Ugliness.* Let us keep alive the belief of beauty ; beauty is not a luxury, it is a necessity.

4. *Death.* The fear we have of death is very real. We should love life and not fear death. The sorrow for a friend's death is most selfish ; we are thinking of ourselves entirely. We should pray for a good death. Comfort comes through everything, sin, sorrow, ugliness and death. Let us cling to our faith in God, in the whole faith, and we shall know that after death there is immortality.

Third Beatitude

" Blessed are the meek for they shall inherit the earth."

The meek or gentle to inherit the earth ! This is a most startling statement, a paradox more than a truth. We could believe it if it said they shall inherit the heaven, as we feel sometimes that the people that were not up to much on earth will be fit for heaven. But when we examine this statement we find that it holds the truth at its very heart, and we begin to see the meaning of it. The characteristic of Jesus that has taken most hold of men is that He is meek, unarmed—Gentle Jesus, we call Him. His whole character is on a par with this meekness. He is unarmed, harmless, not wishing to harm anybody all through His Life. His supreme achievement is to convince men that He not only came to teach the Truth, but that He is the Truth, the Revelation of God the Father. Therefore God is unarmed, harmless, and men have never been able to grasp that truth. Even when He purged the Temple from the money-changers, etc., and used slight, useless force, it was not the force that had any effect as the money-changers were back on Good Friday, but He used it as a symbol.

He was a most positive person, not harmless—taken to mean weak ; He was not a negligible quantity. He made lots of enemies, He frightened the wrongdoers, not because they were afraid of His punishment, but because they were afraid of displeasing Him. He was always talking about Himself : I am the Good Shepherd ; I am the Door ; Come unto Me ; and yet it never grated on His hearers or on us. That was because He was always saying I, I, I, but He always means You, You, You.

Christian meekness is to forget about yourself in

44

your cause. He lost His life that He might find it. We cannot do it. When we talk about ourselves we mean ourselves. Jesus was a fanatic and we must all be fanatics, so long as we are fanatics for a good cause, the Christian cause.

Meekness is the first requisite of moral power. It gives us a glimpse how the meek shall inherit the earth. They wish to serve rather than to dominate and they will lose themselves in the cause, they have entire forgetfulness of themselves, and a yearning desire to develop others.

Jesus is quite fearless and so are all leaders: the completest kind of courage eradicates fear entirely out of our nature. If we do right simply because of fear of the consequences of wrongdoing, we are not redeemed, as we do not do wrong simply out of fear of God or man. Jesus came to show us that, but men could not believe Him, so as He was so meek while on earth they said He would come back in all His glory to judge men, He would gather those who loved Him to Himself, and He would damn the others. They turned the " Gentle Jesus " into an eternal Judge. But Jesus never said anything of the kind. The essence of Christianity is spoiled because of the failure to see Him in His meekness.

We shall not disarm men, until we disarm God in our thoughts. We have armed our Christ, blessed guns and battles, and not seen that we were wrong. We must cling to Jesus and do what He tells us about His meekness. That is not to say that force may not be a necessity at certain times ; if a man goes mad he must be restrained. And there is such a thing as corporate lunacy, and of course that must be stopped on account of others, and to protect the lunatics themselves.

We may have to suffer martyrdom, to follow Christ's

teaching, but we must suffer and not retaliate. We must not be afraid of God, but terrified of life without God on this earth or in the world to come. If the sense of the love of God is withdrawn from man there is no depth to which man cannot sink. Let us transfer our terror of God to terror of life without Him ; let us refuse to remedy failures and disasters by force. Many men want peace because they are afraid of war, but we want peace and we are too brave, not too afraid, to fight for it.

Meekness leads to positive courtesy and good manners. We are told that much of the industrial unrest among the men is due to the manners of the overseers and employers, and thus creates trouble. The reason of that is that they never see anyone but themselves, they see themselves in others, they see others only as relating to themselves.

Meekness leads to the refusal to dominate men, and to the wish to develop them ; there are many signs that it is so. We shall thus become a person without fear, who obeys conventions out of courtesy, a person who cannot be offended.

Fourth Beatitude

" Blessed are those who hunger and thirst for righteousness for they shall be filled."

The Beatitudes give us an impression that they bring us down to the facts of life. There is no blessing for unrealities, for a fool's paradise ; man is blessed when living in the world.

The first Beatitude teaches us that a blessing goes to those who feel and acknowledge their dependence.

The second is that a blessing is on them that face the facts of sin, of sorrow, ugliness and death. These are soft facts, not hard facts. The distinction between hard and soft facts is a great help against realism, and fosters idealism. The soft facts will not last for ever ; there will come a time when there will be no more sin, sorrow, ugliness or death.

Righteousness is a word that has been much misunderstood, because it means so much, and is hard to define. In common with words like Christianity, Socialism, Liberty, it is so difficult to define; it requires too much trouble, so that it has been left out and despised like words that need much pondering over. It goes to the root of our nature, strikes below the reason, is deeper than hunger and thirst, stronger than fear of death. Those are blessed who love righteousness most. Only those souls can grow to fulness, who will drive on to completion of development, to the final completion of human nature for which we are made. Righteousness is an intense desire for harmony, springing out of a great sensibility to discord. So righteousness and peace have kissed each other.

For the sake of examining righteousness we can divide it under three heads : righteousness of head, heart and will.

Righteousness of the head is truth. The intellectual faculties often wake later than the heart and will, especially in women, who only latterly have wakened up in that respect. The hunger of truth is very intense ; it is no good crushing it down in a boy or girl by authority. Christianity definitely gives in this beatitude a blessing to the patient scientific research of truth. But we must beware of credulity. There is need for the white star of righteousness of mind, and the need of following it at all costs. There is a duty of scepticism as well as a duty of faith. Religion collects the facts of the world and makes the hypothesis, then applies the hypothesis to the facts. But in religion there is this difference from science, that it cannot be disproved or be demonstrated. The Christian hypothesis is " God is rational, righteous, reliable." We cannot be too grateful for that, for we escape from a God who is capricious. His Voice speaks to us always, even through the thunder. That there is a conflict between absolute authority and reason is a fact to be taken into account. We cannot forget all that has been discovered about a fact or ignore it, but we must take it into account. Every man must doubt as well as believe. The battle between the facts of good and evil goes on always, and we see it going on on the Cross. But the crucified good rises again, the evil will die, but the good will live on.

Righteousness of the heart. This is an effort to harmonise claims to different things, and our various loyalties. There is the conflict between the loyalty to yourself and your family, or between your family and Church, etc. You are pulled asunder by different loyalties. There is no peace to be obtained unless you make harmony between different loyalties. Nothing is so hard as to find the duty that is nearest to you. We are torn between two loyalties, our duty to the community or to our family, between the Church and the State. We must reduce the conflict by the love of God to some kind of order, and our loyalty to Christ should be placed right away before any other. That is the meaning of that stern saying of Jesus " Whoso hateth not father or mother for my sake is not worthy of me." That is if the conflict is between your mother and Christ your mother must go ; between your child and Christ, your child must go. We must then strike a balance. Righteousness does not belong to a special code, as it must vary ; righteousness comes from the contact with a living Leader, Christ the Lord of the World. The blessing is for those who hunger and thirst for the highest.

Righteousness of the Will. That is righteousness in act, so that you act according to your best desires. " The good that I will I do not, and the evil that I will not, that I do." We must look at the righteousness of Christ. We cannot attain to righteousness by will but only by worship. That which holds your imagination, that which takes possession of you, the living idea, the perfect entire love you have for someone, that which goes below our reason and absorbs us entirely, that is our righteousness, and we can only obtain it by worship. Worship at the blessed Sacrament when He, the Christ, abides in us and we in Him. The worship of Him destroys all bad impulses, makes them impossible, prevents us from wrong, leaves no evil propensity in us. We must always remember that evil is in us, but is not us, we are the sons of God assailed by the evil outside us.

We are very prone to self assertion, but also to self abasement, and the mixture of the two produces often awkward manners ; but we must consecrate both self assertion and self abasement and it will produce a healthy and natural manner. Often self assertion is only self confidence and will never make a good leader.

Christ has revealed to us the highest scales of human values by His character, and has brought everything into harmony and we must follow Him and take His values as our values.

Fifth Beatitude

" Blessed are the merciful for they shall obtain mercy."

It might all be translated into " Blessed be the honest for he shall live in the truth." Mercy conflicts with reality, we consider it a kind of miracle ; mercy is in a strange way in our mind contrary to justice. But mercy is based on a deeper truth about God and man. God is creative love in His essence, and nothing will ever alter His Love ; God is incapable of hurting man, or punishing him, man is His son, His child, and the truth of man is perfection, which perfection will one day be made manifest. Our mistake is that we identify the sinner with the sin ; we call a man a murderer, but no man is only a murderer, he is also a man and a son of God : the punishment is given to the man for the protection of Society. God never identifies the sinner with the sin, He always hates sin, but always loves the sinner, His son, therefore He is always merciful. Our justice is no justice at all, as people are coming to see more and more.

There is a great deal of false mercy in the world ; people call it being charitable and mistake it for mercy ; they do not want to condemn others as they do not want to be condemned themselves.

True mercy is creative love in action, the appeal of truth in God, to truth in man ; the appeal from the highest to the highest. It is coming as a shock to many how little redemptive work our prison system does, although it has much improved. The agony of solitary confinement is so terrible to some natures that it drives them nearly mad ; that is well depicted in Galsworthy's play " Loyalties."

We must strive to avoid identifying the sinner with the sin ; if any one of us is judged by one act our souls are damned. A liar is not a liar, he is a child of God who has fallen and told a lie ; so with every other sin. And we must remember that in damning others we damn ourselves, people who condemn others entirely, deliver judgment on themselves, for if we cannot see God in our neighbour's soul we cannot see Him in our own.

That is the reason Jesus is so down on the Pharisee, as entire condemnation of a man is a denial of the love of God. If there is any sin we can be indignant about it is the sin of pride. Sometimes the only thing to be done to a man who suffers from this is to lash out at him, it works when other things fail and shakes him literally out of his pride. It is what Jesus did in the Temple Court. There is no denying it, we can only be forgiven as we forgive. So many strange doctrines have been woven round the whole doctrine of the Atonement. It was said that God was just and therefore someone had to suffer, so God sent His Son into the world, who suffered for us on the Cross so that we might escape the punishment and be made one with God through the vicarious suffering of Christ. But that is not the whole truth. God loves us, has always loved us, will always love us ; He does not wish or long to punish us, He is outside punishment and sin : it is sin that brings its own punishment. It is active mercy that redeems, seeking the sinner like God seeks us, and justice apart from love is no good. We do not get what we deserve, we are freely forgiven. That word deserve is often untrue. We do not go to hell as a punishment for sin, the sin is the hell, and an unloving person is in hell now, as he lives away from God. When we are self-centred we are in an unhealthy condition, self is in its wrong place, God is the centre, and we only become whole again when we turn to Him. A man may be very prosperous outwardly, possess several motor-cars, and yet he may be in hell, motor cars and all, in the eyes of a Christian. It is the human vindictiveness that went to make the doctrine of hell ; man was jealous of the riches or prosperity of another and went to say that in the future world he would have to suffer for it and go to hell. But God never gave us any authority for that ; away from Him we live in hell, and so this vicious circle is entirely outside Him.

God and Christ are one ; the picture of the Cross is the picture of God and of what sin means to Him. When we show mercy we are getting down to the truth of God. It is not we that do wrong, it is the sin that dwelleth in us ; we love God and are hindered by sin. " O Lord thou knowest that I love thee."

By identifying the sinner with the sin we fix the sin on him and so damn his soul. (The story of Zaccheus which ended with the comforting words " Inasmuch as he also is a son of Abraham.")

It is like fighting a slander, a sin fixed on the sinner. All mercy redeems and restores. This is illustrated by our Lord in the parable of the Prodigal Son.

Sixth Beatitude

" Blessed are the pure in heart for they shall see God."

There are times when we all cry out that there is no God ; the book of Job is full of the lament. The only comfort is that we cannot miss that which we never have had, we miss a vanished hand and voice, but we cannot feel the absence of a thing we have never felt. The explanation is that it is only a mood and that probably for none of us will there be the perpetual vision of God ; there will always be light and darkness, black days and weeks. But when the black days come we must hold fast to the sunshine that is behind them ; the sunshine that once was and will come again. It is impossible to avoid those days of darkness.

That God is there we are perfectly sure, but we must believe it before we can prove it ; you have in every science to believe in a hypothesis before you prove it. What God promised in this Beatitude is that the pure in heart shall be certain of His presence. We get low and discouraged at the times of darkness and call out " Sir, we would see Jesus." We feel that if we had lived when He was on earth we should have clung to Him ; but that was not really so for His contemporaries. Some thought Him mad, some an impostor, and yet some called out to Him " My Lord and my Master," and it is just so now. Some things that are continually before our eyes we never see at all. Men only see what they attend to ; if our attention is only fixed on small things we shall only see small details. The more we see and attend, the more the wonder ought to grow. Attention is voluntary or involuntary ; the latter is mostly found in children and animals, the first only obtained by fixing the attention and educating our involuntary attention, and that is the real true education. The contents of the under-world of your mind will turn your attention to other things, to evil, as it seems to turn naturally to evil. People depict the world as being all grey and drab and evil. Arnold Bennett, for example, takes a grey dull life and is able to make it interesting, and he calls it realism ; but it is not realism truly, as all lives are not dull and grey, nor are all dreary houses in slums ; and even in slums in most dreary looking homes there is plenty of love and courage and even joy. Because the papers are full of divorce cases we begin to think that there is no true love and faithfulness, and we forget the large majority of happy marriages which are not brought to the public notice. A writer on Church History says that from the third century onward there are no more saints, and he quite forgets the quiet, faithful saintly lives of those nobody knew about. All these blot God out of our minds. Some people run to the doctor for the smallest ailment of their body, but they do not mind their minds wallowing in filth and mud.

People will have to come to a saner view, and to a more sensible way of protecting themselves from the infection of the mind. Go to your old-fashioned devotional life, to your Sacraments and cling to them. People say they have grown beyond them, but the truth is they have grown below. Devotion, Worship, Sacraments, those are the ways of protecting your mind from infection. Say your prayers regularly at stated times, get into communion with God, switch your mind into communion with God wherever you are ; cling to the beautiful and the unselfish and you will protect yourself from pollution of the mind. It is Christianity that is realism—it deals with the facts of life.

You know that you see God when your heart is pure, and when your heart is pure you see God and hold communion with Him. You must give your attention to God before you can know Him. We are as certain of the existence of truth and beauty as we are certain that we have feet. Belief in God, seeing God is again a matter of courage, to be brave, to refuse to be frightened by anything, to cling to Him.

Seventh Beatitude

" Blessed are the peacemakers for they shall be called the sons of God."

This is the climax for us ; in 1913 we called peacemakers quiet, inoffensive people, now we fasten with longing on peace ; it is what the world wants and needs, everyone is crying for it, and yet there are still so many war-makers. We long to raise peacemakers.

We notice that this Beatitude comes a long way down the list of Beatitudes, and there is as much in the order as in the substance of the Beatitudes, it is a ladder from earth to heaven, which we have to climb, rung after rung from the bottom, not two steps at a time. There is no such thing as an easy peace ; peace is not cessation of war, it is not negative, it is quite positive. Casting out a devil is not enough, as others may come in. The world is worn, weary, exhausted, it cannot be stirred to enthusiasm by anything, we are blunted and we seem to be drifting rapidly towards disaster. The world cries it does not want war, because they are tired, but that is a wrong basis for any real peace. The world wants a great good without paying the price. The world is full of counterfeits of peace, unions, fellowships, brother-hoods, societies, movements, but they are not true, they are worthless, but not useless, as they include really genuine people who raise the whole movement. These unions with their numberless committees can be made much of if people come in that have the root of the matter in them. Committees only talk, but even that is necessary and useful if the leaders will come forward. Democracy is not government by the mob, but government by the wise by consent of the mob.

The root trouble of all these societies is that people accept with enthusiasm the second commandment, to love their neighbour as themselves. The second commandment is totally devoid of value unless it rests on the first commandment ; the love for my neighbour depends on the love for God.

We say we must love our neighbour as ourselves, but I can love myself as loving God, obeying Him, being in Christ, as I may love myself prosperous and in power, and if I love my neighbour as myself in the last case that love is quite worthless and not even practical. For you cannot share power and riches, etc., with everyone, it would not go round ; so you will share with a few and you will come against a certain section with whom you will not share, against whom you will break out in bitter hatred.

The thing is we have not to be apologetic about religion, or bring it into our life casually (it is not good form!) treating the idea of God like a poor relation that you ask to tea but not to dinner, who is there but not important! No, religion must be everything to you. There is no hope of peace until people have a common sense of high values and of the word of God. You cannot live your life in detail until you have a general plan of life. You cannot be happy unless you are happy about everything.

Peace is the climax of the ladder of the Beatitudes, and you have to climb the ladder, you cannot dash about. We suffer from a torrent of words, but these words are often of no value; there is no other basis for peace but the basis of the ethics of Christ.

We begin by putting off from ourselves the desire of independence, we are poor in spirit, we know we can only find freedom in and through the beloved community, not outside it. We have to search for our life's work, recognise our interdependence, we have to accept the mourning and sorrow, and not seek to escape through a back gate; we have to accept our Cross, bear it and not have a blasphemous anxiety to do God's work, and in order to do that we have to give up fear and become brave people; we must give up fear of breaking the conventions, not become conventionally unconventional. We have to build up in the world an entire desire for truth; lies of every sort have to become abomination; we have to pour into the world the white passion for truth, the loyalty for the highest values, we have to consecrate ourselves saying in our heart: "God, who is giving me the victory," not has given:

we have to have that mercy that believes in man as the son of God, looking at the world with discerning eyes, perceiving what great things our workpeople are capable of ; we have got to have the continuous worship of the Good, the Truth to enable us to see God, and only so can we become peacemakers. And we want to send people like that into the world, quite convinced that you must *be* somebody before you can *do* anything. We can no longer have only one national leader, but we want many leaders, and the Church must send those people into the world fresh from their worship and their Sacraments. You cannot give away what you have not got yourself. There are people who assume that the Church is a failure, the Sacraments not worth coming to ; they refuse the authority of the Church, but they obey implicitly what " they "—meaning nobody in particular—decree.

But stick to your Bibles ; it takes trouble and pain to understand it, but so do all higher values. Those who say Sacraments are no good judge themselves thereby ; they say few go, that the Service is not inspiring, but you will feel it differently if you go to the heart of it. What does it matter if only two or three are there, there are thousands really there although you do not see them. The Bread you eat is not only bread, it means all the material world and binds us all together, and He, our Master, uses It to convey His very Self. It is God Himself. What does it matter if the chemist says its component parts are just the same before their con-secration as after, that does not mean anything. The chemist would say equally of a lovely poem that it is only paper and ink. There is more in It after Consecration : It is my God, It is really God. And if people only do not take the Sacrament as a magical thing but as It really is, a means of communion with

God, it will bring to them and the world at last that Peace of God that passes all understanding.

Eighth Beatitude

" Blessed are those that are persecuted for righteousness sake for theirs is the Kingdom of God."

It is a fact that Christians are called to be in the world but not of it, and that applies to wherever they are. That entails maintaining an impossible balance unless your heart is hid with Christ in God, and unless you lead a devotional life.   Chesterton tells us that it is like a rider riding on two horses (one foot on each) tearing in different directions.   So truth and life is a balance between pitfalls and you cannot maintain your balance unless you pray continually.

> " Let no false confidence betray,
>   No foolish fears mislead,
>   But in the true and narrow way,
>   Be Thou my Guide indeed."

Sometimes there are terrible times when you are a martyr to the Christian faith.   I think we could all die for Christ if He asked us for it, but we have to live for Him, which is far more difficult ; death is easy, life is often hard.

The balance has grown finer now, as it is no longer between the heathen and the Christian we have to choose, but it is between the nominal Christian and real Christianity ; our chief duty is to maintain real Christianity in nominal Christianity.

The persecution may take several forms :—

(1) *Flattery*.   It will cause real pain to a Christian, and will cause you many bitter hours when you get

home. The idea of the people is to propitiate you, or the truth you have spoken, as they agree to it in theory but wish to escape from it in practice. In religion, it is the Cross, the pain, that repels, and yet there is no getting to the heart of Christ except through the Cross. We must however be careful for fear we take gratitude for flattery, and so destroy gratitude. Gratitude ought to bring you to humiliation. How is this to be met? The only answer is that your life must be hid with Christ in God. If you go home pleased with yourself then the world has you, you are beaten and broken by the world.

(2) *Indifference*. That is the second persecution—a pure blank indifference; it seems like a blank wall, and life has nothing to do for you. There is a kind of tacit implication that there is a business world and a natural world, and that Christianity has nothing to do with it. If you condemn this you may be condemning people that are much better than yourself, and yet if you give in you are done, broken.

(3) *Ridicule or Social Ostracism*. There are things that a Christian cannot touch, about which he cannot compromise, as for instance gambling, and his abstaining from it brings upon him ridicule. There is an assumption among people that what is new is right. Take a jazz band : if people knew the origin of jazz they would absolutely shun it, but as it is in the fashion, if you will not listen to it you are sneered at, you are told that nothing wholesome can be artistic, that to see beauty in innocent things belongs to the Victorian era, etc. etc. We may, and must, set our face against it, but it is difficult to keep the balance. There are many temptations that assail you when you want to keep this balance :—

(1) To lose your sense of value. There comes a time

when Christianity becomes unreal, and may permanently remain so, and the things of the world seem real. We must fight against that for all that we are worth ; atmosphere is more than words. There are to me entertainments that are so vile, the atmosphere is so bad, that we should avoid them at all costs. Now the theatre and other entertainments are quite different. As long as we feel we could pray while at an entertainment the atmosphere is wholesome, but when we cannot pray we had better come out at once.

(2) To lose our temper. We always regret it afterwards ; we say cutting things and wish we had not said them. It may be necessary sometimes to show wrath, but few are fit for that. What we must do is to explain patiently what has been wrong, we must not touch it personally, we must be firm but loving.

(3) To be a prig. You will always be called a prig if you set up a higher standard, but you will be a prig if you take joy in persecution and it gives you a sense of enlarged personality ; it enlarges you, not your Lord. There ought always to be a sense of pain in persecution, joy and pain together. You may and will become a prig unless your life is hid with Christ in God, unless you cling to your devotional life.

(4) Compromise.

(5) Despair. You go home and pity yourself, you say you know you are a failure, and all is dark. The only comfort you will have is that your Lord has been with you. Then cling fast to Him. My Lord, My Lord, why hast Thou forsaken Me ?

(6) Getting a delusion of persecution. This is quite a common idea ; it often arises from a desire to be with the sinners and do like them. They think they are unwanted, unloved, but the thought only exists in their imagination.

The Beatitudes

There are finally three things we must learn :—

(1) *Recollection*. Recall yourself to yourself. There must be a Church at the back of your mind and you must be able, wherever you are, to call yourself to your little Chapel and there commune with God. It must be there always as we cannot live the Christian life without. There must be in you something more than your words, a personality that is behind your words. Therefore you must practise recollection.

(2) *Continual prayer*. People say it is impossible, but it is not only prayer in words, but the attitude of mind that turns to God, and takes all our difficulties and anxieties to Him.

(3) *Definite discipline of life*. We all have a skeleton rule of life ; that should be the minimum, but we clothe that skeleton rule with flesh and blood, and endeavour to go beyond the minimum. Say you pray twice a day and go to Communion once a week, that is only the minimum.

What it all comes to in the end is that we must have communion with Christ, that communion getting clearer and brighter. Sometimes we wish we could get away, but He will not let us go. He has firmer hold of us than we have of Him.

* These are manifestly skeleton notes ; but they must stand as they are, for it would not do for someone else to attempt to clothe them with flesh and blood.—EDITOR.

The Prologue to S. John's Gospel

Chap. 1, verses 1–14

First Address

THIS passage which is used by the Priest after Mass should be a subject of constant meditation to him for it embodies the whole of the Christian Religion.

In this first address, before we consider our subject, our main task is to arrive at such a state of mind that our meditations may be fruitful. There are two states of mind, never quite complete, between which all men waver :

1st. That state when everything matters, and matters very much.

2nd. That state when nothing matters at all.

To rest in the last state is to suffer spiritual death, it is a highly dangerous state to be in (when life is for ever fighting against the spiritual death and we descend to the bottomless abyss from which God called us), and the nearest approach to hell, it leads finally to madness.

The first state is that of the highest spirituality. Sometimes it is said that there is an antagonism between work and worship, and that a busy life cannot be spiritual, but the life of the most busy or spiritual men give the lie to that statement. All spiritual people have lived busy, active lives.

Look at Our Lord's life. The first part of His life was spent as a busy working carpenter, in the second part He was continually thronged by crowds and had no time for sleep or food.

Or take S. Paul's life. Or S. Thomas Aquinas, whose books would fill a shelf and were all written by his own hands. Or Wesley, or General Booth (a genuine mystic).

There is no antagonism between work and worship, and the real contemplators are very active, but through their life is a determination to worship. They feel they have not time *not* to worship, as all their energy and work is frittered away if it is not built on prayer and worship, and the only way to do rapid and efficient work is to do it on a basis of inward peace ; through their life runs the rhythm of prayer. The Collect for the Fourth Sunday after Trinity illustrates this ; we pray to be delivered from the "*fear.*" It is fear and pride that prevent rapid work.

Although every day ought to be consecrated and holy there is need for special times like Retreats, to hallow the daily round, the common task. And people who preach the doctrine that special times of prayer are not necessary do not practise prayer, as there is no agreement between real life and experience to support their statement.

It is impossible to attend to everything in this world in which we live, and we have to make a selection, and only attend to those things which appeal specially to our temperaments, and so make an impression on us. We are all born with special temperaments, some balanced, equable ; most of us develop a deformed soul of one kind or another. So at certain times and places we determine to give ourselves to the contemplation of the beautiful and good in its highest form, we have special times to find God, so that having found Him there, we will find Him everywhere, as our God is always omnipresent, whether it is God, or money, or golf.

So a Retreat is not useless when we voluntarily shut out other things and contemplate that which is beautiful and get a vision of God which will not fail us wherever we go. We cannot learn to pray always until we pray sometime; we cannot confine our God to the Sacrament, or localise Him there, He is omnipresent; but having found Him there we consecrate all our work, and all other things to Him, and we find Him omnipresent in all we undertake. So we defend Retreats and the Feasts of the Church. We forget that Christmas, Good Friday, Easter, Ascension, are all different views of the same truth, and that they must all be brought into every day of our life.

It is possible for our worship to be disconnected from the rest of our life, if we make it an end in itself. It is only a means to a great end: "That we finally may so pass through things temporal that we may reach to things eternal," which does not only mean that we pass through this life to the life beyond, but also that we may find that life Eternal here in this world. "All willeth and worketh together to that end."

Set your affections on things above; do not only see the beauty of the lily but lift your eyes beyond the lily to see Him who made it. The end of a Retreat is that things temporal may be tinged with the life eternal. Nothing that a priest, or anyone says or does, ever brings a soul to God. He must come Himself and approach the soul.

At the beginning of this Retreat we should not make great resolutions to conquer this or that; it would be wasting precious time; the main part of our time should be taken getting near to God, and seeking His strength, and then making resolutions. The more we can rest and trust Him, the better our time will be spent. Let us not torment ourselves that we have lost similar chances before, and so be despondent; all progress is disappointing, but let God judge, do not judge yourself. Let yourself go entirely beyond the Temple and see what is behind it, and then go out and let the Retreat do its work and let it lead to more pity, charity, mercy and a braver heart.

Second Address

" In the beginning was the Word, and the Word was with God, and the Word was God."

In his prologue S. John tries to express the inexpressible, he swings right back out of time and space, so to speak, to the beginning of Eternity, to the world of " I am," and he brings us to the ultimate reality of all things. At present people are very fond of saying they like practical teaching, plain preaching of plain truth, but that takes us nowhere, it leaves us in our own small selves, and it cannot help us as it does not go to the root of the matter, but only deals with the symptoms. We need that teaching the least as we can only live aright as we live the whole life, and come to the knowledge of the truth. We can only make a selection of the many things that claim our attention, and we so often make such a poor selection, that the mean things we have selected take all our attention and we do not notice God. We miss Him because we have not trained our attention for the big things of life, so S. John turns our attention to the big Truth. In the beginning was the Word—Logos. Logos means two things :—

1st. It means the part of me, the reason, that can

communicate with you. It tells us that in the heart of the Eternal there is something akin to me, something that can communicate with me ; that God is like man, and man like God ; something that responds in man to God. We must cling to that Faith firmly, whatever the world may seem to be.

2nd. Logos, means the expression of the outward and visible sign of the Sacrament of Speech.

Not only is there reason in God, but also the present power to express it. The use of the term Logos means that in the beginning God was self-conscious ; conscious of the Truth and anxious to express it. Of His very Essence He did create, express, communicate Himself. He was Love. When a poet has written a poem, that poem lives for him, and brings him back the joy he has lost sometime in a moment of depression. So we are God's poem, His creation, and we can sing back our joy to Him. God is like ourselves.

S. John tries to express the inexpressible, he tries to express what he has felt himself, his own experience. Nowadays truth, except scientific truth, which can be proved, is at a discount, and yet has scientific truth had the deepest influence on our life ; have not the mystic and the spiritual truths had more influence on the world and the life of men ? The Word was with God and the Word was God. S. John repeats that unity is in difference and difference in unity. He is trying to express, and does convey to us that at the same time God is not known and yet well known, in fact the doctrine of the Trinity. He cannot formulate this doctrine in positive words, but he tries to protect and defend it from small views of small people. God in Himself is beyond our ken, no picture one can draw is ultimately adequate and yet he wants to show us the transcendence of God. We need continually to remember that God is immense, awful in the real sense of the word. We need to learn that life without awe is incomplete. We are little people, living in a little world and we like a little God, and that is a great danger. We look at life in a topsy-turvy way, always turning to the origin of life, instead of looking at the immensity of life; our practical life is hedged in with ignorance, the big things are beyond our reach. Great men do not feel the same, they see the wonders and are filled with awe. We need to keep a sense of God's immensity, to bow down and say, my Lord and my God—God the Counsellor, all wise, the Prince of Peace; but He will never be the Prince of Peace to us until we see Him as the Counsellor, the Almighty. That we should believe that God is transcendent is the first thing, but it would depress us if we did not know that the Word was at the beginning.

THE COMRADE GOD

Thou who dost dwell in depths of timeless being,
    Watching the years as moments passing by,
Seeing the things that lie beyond our seeing,
    Constant, unchanged, as æons dawn and die;

Thou who canst count the stars upon their courses,
    Holding them all in the hollow of Thy hand,
Lord of the world with its myriad of forces
    Seeing the hills as single grains of sand;

Art Thou so great that this our bitter crying
    Sounds in Thine ears like sorrow of a child?
Hast Thou looked down on centuries of sighing,
    And, like a heartless mother, only smiled?

Since in Thy sight to-day is as to-morrow,
    And while we strive Thy victory is won,
Hast Thou no tears to shed upon our sorrow?
    Art Thou a staring splendour like the sun?

Dost Thou not heed the helpless sparrow's falling?
    Canst Thou not see the tears that women weep?
Canst Thou not hear Thy little children calling?
    Dost Thou not watch above them as they sleep?

Then, O my God, Thou art too great to love me,
    Since Thou dost reign beyond the reach of tears,
Calm and serene as the cruel stars above me,
    High and remote from human hopes and fears.

Only in Him can I find home to hide me,
    Who on the Cross was slain to rise again;
Only with Him, my Comrade God, beside me,
    Can I go forth to war and sin and pain.

The term Logos bids us remember that God is unknowable and yet that we can know Him, and trust Him,
and that He is infinitely worth knowing. We have kinship
with God. We are on firm ground when we trust our
highest values and look at a thing and say that is goodness, beauty. Jesus is God's concrete expression of the
highest values. The proposition of the Trinity is a
question of value. Jesus is God because He is the best
person we know and S. John means this when he says:
The Word is God and yet not God. Though beyond
us, God is always of the same kind; God is more tender
and loving and self sacrificing than Jesus, never less.
God is expressed in the highest we can know, so our
highest values are the true values. Goodness is something of absolute value, and only as we lay hold of it
do we get to the root of life. People want to work the
whole of life in terms of pain and pleasure. Once we
judge or live on the level of social utility our souls are
damned.

We must trust the highest values and believe that
faithfulness, constancy, are good in themselves. Hatred
is wrong because it is not of God. As we cling to
absolute values we attain to peace about God. When

Jesus and God are One there comes upon us an urgent spirit driving us out to change the world, and that is the real meaning of the Trinity.

When Father and Son are one in our hearts, and we feel Jesus ascended in our hearts, then we realise the world belongs to Jesus and everything in it. God who is transcendent and who is a dominating, guiding Spirit, is one with Jesus. The life of the Spirit only begins when we have grasped the Ascension and only then when we long to be like Him.

This is the devotional meaning of the Trinity. All the doctrines are crystallisations of the deep experience of men ; there is something behind the doctrines. We cannot do without dogmas. God is very friendly : He has not left us alone but He is always striving in us, and that is our faith, and by that faith we live.

Third Address

"Through Him all things were made that were made."

God is in things. God made the things through the Logos or reason, therefore there is a meaning in things ; nature is not alien to ourselves, it is sense ; we may not understand it all but there is a reason behind it. That is the Christian faith. Evidence of this truth is :—

(1) The deep feeling of kinship ; behind nature there is something friendly. Many people feel it very keenly, but some people do not feel it much, and it may nearly be lost. In the trenches it was little felt, but it could be recalled by such a small thing as a poppy.

If you analyse the feeling of beauty you will find that beauty is the relation between men and things ; sometimes it is said that it is in the eye of the beholder more than in the thing itself, but it is the relation between the two. In the 23rd Psalm the sheep did not follow

the shepherd because of the beauty of the pasture, but
because they wanted food; also it was not the beauty
of the pool that attracted them, but they wanted to
drink. Men, like animals, in the lower stage, look at
things as they can use them, but that feeling is soon
supplanted first by gratitude. The animals are first for
the use of men, but we should have a feeling of gratitude
to them, and we can pass to a state where there is just
the beauty we notice. A millionaire may buy a picture
but all he thinks of is the price he paid for it, and the
thought that it belongs to him—he may not understand
its beauty. The beauty is the joy in things, and we
should hear the call of God through things.

(2) Evidence. The discovery of order in things is
the second evidence. Men have brooded over things
till they have found that there is order in them; every
star is governed by immutable laws. Darwin examined
ants for ten years and his observations helped him in
evolving the theory of evolution which has been such a
help to our knowledge of the growth of the world and
of the animals which live in it. The discovery of that
order and beauty have made us look for God in the
normal things of life, not only in rare phenomena.

Many people feel a great difficulty in the fact that along-
side all the beauty there is, in nature, so much cruelty,
disease, waste, one animal preying on another, and they
feel that God who allows it all cannot be the kind God.
But when we think of these facts (and we should face
facts) in relation to God we must always bear in mind
that pain is very relative. What is torture to a sensitive
woman is hardly inconvenience to a navvy and would
hardly tickle a mussel. When a dog cries with pain
he may not feel pain, but only call for protection.
Nature has anæsthetics of its own. Hardly any pain is
felt in battle, only after the battle. The idea of pain in

animals is not what ought to prevent us being cruel to them, it is the gratitude we owe them for their self-sacrifice that makes us kind to them. Ingratitude in anything is damning to the soul. The idea of cruelty ought not to spoil our joy in nature's beauty ; we ought not to add and pile up all the pain of all animals ; every one only bears one pain.

Next to the revelation of God in person comes the revelation of God in things.

Fourth Address

" In Him was the Life and the life was the light of men"; and the light shineth in darkness and the darkness cannot swallow Him up."

S. John passes from the revelation of God in things to the revelation of God in men, in history. In animals it is the first glimmer, in men it passes on to dawn. God is seen more clearly in man, there is in him a higher revelation and meaning ; light has dawned in the mind of man.

When we search for a meaning in life we come face to face with the problem of evil.

(1) There has been a growth, a progress. In that God has done so much, there has been wonderful progress in beauty and growth ; man has grown from strange beginnings to his present stature. This fact ought to make us very thankful for what God has done.

(2) Throughout all this development there are signs that there has been a retrograde movement, bringing on disease, failure.

There are then either two things to face—the mystery of evil if you believe in God and His Love, or the mystery of good if the world is not a God-made world.

The problem of evil is the most insoluble problem in the world ; the Bible gives no solution, and we must recognise that it cannot be solved ; and that is only natural because if it could be solved you would find a meaning in it, a reason, a logos, and in that case God would have made it, which cannot be as He is all good. So evil is not rational and cannot be explained. God did not will it, that we are certain of, and our business is not to explain it but to destroy it. Jesus came to destroy it.

Some people say that the good of evil is to keep us struggling, but we are dead unto sin and alive unto God in righteousness. That is our destiny, and until we want to get rid of sin, we cannot live in God. It is this living in God which is the Life of Grace ; living in Grace lifts us above the conflict. We can grow in measure and do right because we have surrendered to the life of God.

God's Will for us is to be one with Him and with our fellow men. Evil endeavours to make us live independent of God and fellow men.

The animals cannot refuse the self-sacrifice, they cannot choose, but we can refuse the sacrifice. Our destiny is to serve God and man, to give all the time and give, and give, but we can refuse. This refusal is the root of all sin. To imagine that we can be independent of others and only think of ourselves and our pleasures and to forget that the willing sacrifice is the true purpose of life.

Man's first idea is to use God for his own ends, that is idolatry. Man originally prayed to his idol for success in battle, and if he was not successful he broke up his idol. Idolatry is using God to serve men's desires, and resenting when He will not do their will. Idolators do not give themselves to God, they want God for their own purposes; they try to use God, to change His Will, instead of conforming their will to God's Will. So-called " good works " are sometimes not good, but bad if they are undertaken in the wrong spirit, i.e. from the desire to be well thought of, to be praised, to be with a special set of people. Work done in that spirit makes them fretful, worried, as they resent any criticism or blame, and they have no joy in their work, and they wonder why the work goes all wrong. If they have given themselves entirely to their work from the right motive and only think of the work, not of themselves, if they listen to criticisms they will find out if they are just, and if so they will alter their method; if they are unjust they will do nothing as it does not matter.

It is no good trying to use God just for our purpose. The Jews all through their history tried to do it; prophet after prophet told them they were wrong and that the meaning of life is to give, not to get, until Isaiah in the 53rd Chapter reaches the highest watermark of the Old Testament and reaches to the level of the New and the coming of Christ, showing that the meaning of life is willing sacrifice. When pain comes, as it must, God gives us power to bear it and to transmute it into peace and joy. If we look for justice in this world we shall not find it, as not only are good people not spared pain, but they often suffer more than others, but they count it their proudest privilege, their greatest joy; they take their share of sin-bearing and suffering and are proud of it, for we are called to give. To give, to take trouble to give and be nice to other people is what makes the world go round, it is one way of expressing love.

The bit that will cause you worry is the bit of your

will you want to keep, not to yield to God. Then take it in your two hands and give it to God and you will have peace.

Fifth Address

"The Word became Flesh."

Christ would have come to us whether we had sinned or not. He is the coping stone of God's plan of creation. God laid hold of human nature and taking it, used it to speak to man in terms of humanity. This new life is the completion and redemption of human life. By giving us a God-centred life God completes us. He is the culmination of the process of evolution. He comes to make us at one with God and in so doing He destroys sin. We don't hold that all other religions are false, but in Christ we find all that is true in other religions. The Incarnation is the crowning of a process taking place all over the world. The whole world was ringed round with a call to something to come and save it. Light dawned when Christ came to save us in answer to the call.

Revelation of God—a Life, always coming through everything, striving to find expression. Restless energy, always seeking. God seeks us day by day. We remember this when we are tempted to evil but forget when we are tempted to good and refuse. God knocks again and again at our hearts and we slam the door in His Face.

God seeks me. I believe this with all the power of my being (cf. sea beating against a rock), c.f. God beating at our hearts now in Retreat and we are come preparing to listen and rest in Him. When He became Flesh He took the whole human nature, not only the body. The

Word took human nature and through it expressed Divinity. I do not know myself, I have no idea what I am in God's sight. It is a distortion of Incarnation to suppose that Jesus knew He was King of Kings when a Babe. He had to work out this knowledge by ordinary human means. He had a mind, feeling, thoughts like ours. He had doubts as we have, and was tempted as we are. He had to wrestle, fight, as I have, but I have Him with me. What He did and said we are meant to do and say through Him, but what He was we can never hope to be. He was not an ordinary man like Shakespeare, if He were I have no chance of Salvation ; He is always human and divine at the same time. He breaks no laws, but goes to the heart of laws and uses them in miracles. His means of knowing what He was is the same as my means of knowing what I am through Him. The study of psychology is an amazing confirmation of the Divinity of our Lord. I am driven more and more to His Feet by every psychological textbook. We thank God that He came and comes : " The Word was made flesh."

Sixth Address

What is that flesh that He took ? I am going to try and describe to you the machinery that He had and we have also.

What machinery does depends on what is put into it. Psychology only describes the machinery, not the product. God uses the machinery. God comes along the same road as the devil does.

Psychology describes the machine, Religion is what you put into the machine, the Grace of Our Lord Jesus Christ. Some psychological conclusions are only tentative, have not yet been tested, so it is rather dangerous to dabble in it unless you can give your life up to the study of it.

Discovery of the Unconscious. The unconscious mind moves your limbs, following out the subconscious intention fixed there by habit. Hypnotism (cf. man who danced on his hat). Man did the action at a certain time, calculated when he should do it, but had no recollection of having been told to do it. Our conscious mind is the smallest part of our mind.

Description of the Machinery. We are like proprietors of a furnished room with one window brightly polished looking out on a street. At the back of the room is the furniture, tools rusting from want of use. Behind that there is a dark chamber we know nothing about; memory pictures are here that we don't like. It is all one room, the least important part is the bright part by the window.

The dark inner chamber (the unconscious) is the most important; our memories are there, it is a store-house of impressions, unforgotten. They may be repressed so that we can't call them up at will but they are there. No memories are lost. They all go into that dark room. Wandering thoughts come from there and gusts of temper. The further back you put them in the room the more trouble they are to you. The most dangerous thing is a repressed evil picture. You say you have a bad memory; no one has a bad memory, it depends on how you are able to fish the old things out! There is a very close connection between this part of your mind and your body, e.g. woman cured of cancer but not cured of the cause which was resentment against her husband. The conscious mind, the bright part by the window, is in communication of course with the unconscious mind, the dark chamber. Your instincts dwell in this back room too, instinct to eat, fight, fly ; you act on these ; to repress them is to court disaster. Habits are also formed here. Control and government of the " unconscious mind " is most important in the education of the spiritual life. This " unconscious " is plastic, it can be trained, educated and redeemed ; if left alone it can do awful things. It is open to impressions, is retentive, stores things. It is dark and the abode of the primitive and animal. The next part, the room dimly lit (the *fore-conscious*), is what you go into when you day-dream. There the most wonderful things are born, art, music, inspiration. These make or mar you. All great things are born there. This fore-conscious is the road between the unconscious (dark room) and the conscious (the bright slit by the window). We don't notice the " fore-conscious " enough. To get into the way of using this part and not abusing it, is very important.

The Slit by the window. Here you can begin to make impressions. You can send things to be stored in the back room. Julian of Norwich said repeatedly " all shall be well." It is very important to set the tone of the impressions, to have a general formula to repeat like " all shall be well, thanks be to God " or bits of Psalm 23, instead of phrases like " it's sickening," " it's too bad." Ejaculatory prayer sets the tone of impressions. A truth that comes in through the window of consciousness goes right through all the parts of the machinery of the mind, runs underneath and comes out again in conduct. The person who dwells constantly on the love of God will get inward peace. The Word, the Christ, the Logos is what we must put into our machinery. Putting Him in is what matters. Always your thought must turn back to that. The machinery is good and it will work, only we must use it rightly, not only for our own comfort. Our centre to which we return must bring us nearer Christ. The last thing at night, the first thing in the morning is the time to set the tone of impressions in your fore-consciousness by some formula.

Seventh Address

" And dwelt among us."

Jesus used that machinery of His Mind to express God, so we must use our machinery in the same way with His help. We must supply our mind, feed it with the Bread of Life. The Word " dwelt among us." His Death on Calvary was the culmination of His Life. We can't separate the Atonement from the Incarnation. He could never have died that Death unless He had lived that Life, every step of which was sacrifice.

We will now try to go behind the Gospel narrative and discover our Lord's devotional private life; what He privately thought necessary attention to higher things. Because if it was necessary for Him, how much more so for us.

(1) Jesus Christ was a constant attender at Church, He went regularly to the Synagogue. Nowadays people want to pray alone, they say they will go to Church only when it is empty. Jesus didn't think so. You can't feed that machinery of yours with the best unless you are a member of an institution with history behind it. Jesus accepted the tradition of the Church but made it His own. It is not possible to cut ourselves off from the past. We cannot cast away ceremonies and sacramental acts that have been handed down to us. We need authority, a rich inheritance, to be the food of our minds. There is great worth psychologically, in ceremonial acts of worship joined in with others. Each one of us is the Church expressed at a point. You

cannot overrate the fact of your weekly attendance at Mass.

(2) Jesus was constantly studying the Scriptures. He used His fore-conscious mind to bring it to His unconscious. He meets the problem of hunger (when tempted) by " Man shall not live by bread alone," etc. He has His general formula ready. It was the same with other temptations also, He was ready with His formula because He has brooded, pondered over it. The worth of making yourself familiar with the text of the Bible cannot be overestimated. In our reading (i.e. lessons for the day) ponder over some of it.

(3) Jesus' practice of prayer. He prayed all night at a Crisis. His prayer was not beseeching, more like day-dreaming, fixing His mind on God's Love. A great mystic said : Never look over much at your difficulties, look over their shoulders at that which is behind . . . The Face of Jesus. We need to pray especially at morning and night ; it has been said " The fate of the day depends how you spend the first quarter of an hour and the last." What kind of thoughts do you close the day with ? " Father into Thy hands I commend my spirit " may have been Jesus' night habit, His night formula. Running through His Life is that perpetual habit of day-dreaming, brooding over things. He has not been idle. It is better to day-dream like Jesus than to let your worries take hold of you, and brood over them. Suppose He dreams over a door which He is planing in the carpenter's shop, He ponders over it. " I am the Door " comes out later in His Ministry. " It is finished." I think He had often said that when He had finished a good piece of work, stood and looked at it and said just that. He was always a thoughtful person about common things. Day-dreaming is a practical thing. Nothing ruins work as much as

friction inside. Some of the greatest Saints have been very practical in their work. Fuss is the enemy of work. We all spend a lot of time in thinking of nothing in particular, our business is to train ourselves to think of the things that matter. Behind Jesus' life there was this quiet life of His. He did not suppress His instincts. He lifted them up. He took His instincts and made them minister to His Revelation of God. Don't repress and cut out, but uplift and sanctify—" sublimate " your instincts. Let us take all the riches of Christ, make that our soil and grow things on it. Supply the machinery of your mind with this and you will grow.

Eighth Address

" And we beheld His glory."

Some did and some did not. There was the tragedy of His Life. He was crucified between the thief He saved and the thief He did not save. Many more saw Him than we know of. There is an illuminating story of one who saw : Zacchæus. He was a publican, he collected monies, made what he could out of it, within the limits of violent extortion in which the Government supported him. He was grasping, wanted to get more, yet he wanted to stand well with the people. Part of his character was repressed ; underneath he wanted to be saved, there was a vein of tenderness which he suppressed. He had done well, was known for a hard man who always crushed down the better and nobler side of him. S. Matthew's throwing up his work and following Jesus worried Zacchæus dreadfully. You can see him adding up his accounts and wandering thoughts coming all the time : two and two are four. What *made* Matthew do it ? Bother. Nine and seven.

Who is this Jesus? and so on. He day-dreams; his repressed instincts cry out to him and the sum is "I want to see Jesus." Now he knows the crowd won't let him get near Jesus, he is hated and feared. So we can see the little fat man's thoughts. Suddenly it occurs to him, "I used to climb trees when I was a boy. I will climb trees again," and he does. Directly he is seen he is spoken against. Jesus' first instinct on over-hearing him slandered is "What can I do for him?" So He says "Come down, I'm going to have dinner with you." Zacchæus is at once won by this friendliness. He shouts, "I will give half my goods to feed the poor." He immediately must do something for Jesus. But the crowd laugh, so he doubles his statement and the crowd laughs again incredulously, they know him. He is not believed and he breaks his heart until Jesus says, "Salvation is come to this house," etc. Zacchæus is completely changed on seeing Jesus, he has found someone on whom he can rest all his instincts, he need no longer repress them. He still wants to stand well with someone but it is with God. If you would see Jesus you must always make a venture, be a little peculiar, but be sure it is in the right way. We have to be reckless with ourselves in the service of Jesus Christ.

Compare Judas, a man who didn't "see" Jesus. He was greedy, self-assertive, because he was clever; he wanted to dominate; he could bamboozle himself without limit, his cleverness was a snare. He made Jesus a tool by which he used his bad instincts of domination. He wanted to manage Jesus and the other disciples. He pretended to himself that it was necessary for him to dominate (see S. John vi. end of chapter). His ambition was that when Jesus came into His Kingdom, he, Judas, should be the Chancellor of the Exchequer. S. Peter is a jumble of instincts, the rather stupid ordinary man. Jesus looks across at Judas and says, " Have I not chosen you twelve and one of you is a devil ? " He knows what is going on in Judas all the time. He tries him again at the last moment when He says " He that dippeth with Me in the dish shall betray Me." Judas must face his repression and lay himself at Jesus' feet or reject his good instincts, and that is what he does. We hope he goes mad ; the good left in him may have driven him mad, his repressed good instincts. He deceived himself and that is what we must not do. We must have the naked eye ; all instincts can be made good. If only Judas could have managed for Jesus. Absolute honesty is necessary and the consecrating and lifting up of your talents to God.

Another comparison is Pilate. He was like rather an incomplete Lord Mayor, a fussy, self-sufficient little man, whose ruling instinct was fear, fear of losing his position. Pilate and his wife were both afraid, afraid of Jesus too. Pilate's fear breaks out in irritability ; when driven to make a decision he washes his hands, puts it on to someone else, he is afraid. (You always blame other people for the faults you fear in yourself—that is called projection.) If I were to get you to talk unreservedly about your neighbour to me for half an hour, I should know your fears. So we have seen one set of people saw His glory, they were the honest ones, and the others deceived themselves and didn't see. We must have absolute honesty with ourselves.

Ninth Address

" And we beheld His glory."

They saw and were never the same again. They

" saw " the glory as of the only begotten of the Father
and it changed their lives. By the naked power of His
personality He stands gigantic over the moral world ;
He holds supremacy. He achieved this among the Jews
who were a monotheistic people ; it was their pride
that they worshipped one God only ; He showed something to them which made them put Jesus on the level
with Jehovah, though it was too bright for them to
grasp. Jesus came to crown or reveal the truth in its
fulness. He forced them to believe that He revealed to
them the nature of God. Their relationship to the
universe changed altogether.

(1) They learned that the only power in the world is
Love ; it was a new idea to them ; their God was fierce,
the God who scourged people. Love was dawning,
mercy and compassion too, but He was always an armed
God to the prophets. It was quite a new idea to them
to worship something helpless with no power to drive ;
it made them desire to make Him the equal of God. God
who came down to win men emptied Himself. It was
a staggering revelation to them that God should humble
Himself, that He should lead and not drive. It was
topsy turvy to them ; their God was on the throne with
a sword. Here came one naked, helpless and alone,
but with extraordinary spiritual power. They could
not grasp it, so they gave Him throne, swords and
judgments in heaven because He would not have them
on earth. He had shewn them a new world, but they
wrestled between that and the old world idea. They
tried to make Him the far-off God of the Old Testament
as well as the God of love. The truth that God is like
Jesus, that is the tremendous conviction that changed
men's lives. Power means ability to carry out a purpose. Before you talk of God's power, you must know
His purpose. His purpose is the perfection of a living

creature. His final power is the spiritual power of love revealed through Jesus Christ. The more we act on this, the more progress we make : e.g. as we cease to beat children we learn to win them. All great men of the Christian community have been great lovers. "Little children love one another"; more was done by that than by storms and violence.

(2) They learned a new doctrine of suffering; those who serve Him best will suffer most. The news that God suffered was amazing to them. When Jesus told S. Peter that He must suffer, he could not understand. "You are thinking of old world ideas," says Jesus, "Kings don't sit on thrones now, they bear burdens, they suffer." This brought S. Paul up short at the gate of Damascus. "I am Jesus whom thou persecutest." Persecuting God was a new idea. He had had a glimmer of it before on S. Stephen's face when he was being stoned. He had always thought suffering was God's punishment, it was new to him to make the Suffering Servant the equal of God. The great people in the world are not those called to high positions, but those called to suffer and who do suffer and are crowned with gold shaped like thorns, though they dare not wear a real crown of thorns because Jesus was the only One who did.

(3) They learned that true dignity meant humility and loving service. Serving communities were formed, charity and humility being their foundation. They learned that to stand on your dignity is to make a fool of yourself. We spoil and ruin ourselves trying to be dignified otherwise than by loving service.

(4) They learned that love was the secret of severity, that God was eternally longing for them, but they read in His words the description of the awful consequences on those who went astray. It isn't He who wills the world

should suffer, it is that evil is the world. There is an evil world outside God, but His Face is above it. God is pure love through Jesus. I cannot be afraid of Him, but I am terrified of life without Him. When man gets away from God individually there is no depth to the awfulness to which he will sink. Hell is a reality but not God's will. Hell is the consequence of living away from God. The glory of God is that He came to lift us out of Hell.

(5) They learned the splendour of sacrifice. They saw Him crucified and learned that God was love, that God is like Jesus. Even as you look into the future and look at the Judgment Day. When He comes He will be the same Jesus, unchanged, weak, helpless, quietly, full of love as ever, with the same wounds, the same marks of the Cross, suffering. He will not be changed, but we shall be. We shall have learned that we ought to glorify and crown Him with seven crowns, because He is the Truth. There is no other glory save that of the Cross which is the Glory of Love. The Church is trying to glorify the Lamb to-day in elaborate glories of worship in the Mass. Only as we learn to worship that which we do not fear and that which can only uplift us, are we truly redeemed. The Christian is one who suffers, loves and serves and finds both joy and peace. The Carpenter will come again, wearing, as before, His working jacket underneath as all men do.

Tenth Address

"Full of grace and truth."

There has been a great theological controversy as to the authorship of S. John's Gospel. It was written at the end of the Christian era long after the other gospels. It is of a much richer Christian experience due to a longer

" pondering over " Jesus.   S. John sees a larger and a deeper Christ, if tradition be true that he wrote his gospel at the end of a very long life.   How his hand would tremble with awe as he wrote " In the beginning " ;   " There is a spirit that abideth."   S. John teaches us more of the Holy Spirit because he understood better and was filled with Him.

" Full of grace and truth."   I know this, says S. John, by experience.   (Jesus came down from God and through the flesh worked His way back to God.   Directed day-dreaming and meditation.)   Other people died and passed on and their memory dims and darkens, but the memory of Jesus remains because of His Spirit and He grows ever nearer as the years go on (c.f. Saints burnt for love of Him, though the disciples forsook Him when He was on earth).   As we advance in years and knowledge we never get beyond Jesus, we grow to see Him in everything more and more.   What did this " Grace " do ?   It became a power of new life, new love, the fellowship of the Holy Spirit.   This fellowship of Christ spread all over the whole Roman Empire from Palestine to Spain.   Historians tell us how they saw people coming out with lanterns in their hands, kneeling in the snow and singing " O Lamb of God that takest away the sins of the world," having bound themselves to the service of gentle love.   They broke bread and separated in fear of their lives.   These fellowships were the choicest fruit of the Grace of God. What His Spirit did was to make the Church grow. Fellowship is the life of a body of brethren whose hall-mark is its power to create a bond of union between soul and soul so that one and one make more than two because it is two plus Him which is infinite.   The central fact of the fellowship is the breaking of bread because He told them to.   They consecrated the bread and wine which became His body and blood, thereby guaranteeing His presence among them. This is intellectually sound ; it is nearer the truth to say " This is His Body " than to say " It is bread and wine," they are the vehicles, channels, that He takes to come into our souls. It is what His body was here on earth, a vehicle, channel. As we kneel we are in His presence, that is the power, the centre of Christianity, there is no magic there. *How* we come is what matters : thousands missed Him before and thousands miss Him now. The Blessed Sacrament is the centre of a sin-bearing fellowship. It needs no Sacrament to make God love us, He could never cease to do that ; but it takes something to bring that love home to us. Through the fellowship you get it by the power of the Sacraments (c.f. in absolution too, the power in His Church to forgive sins). The Priest represents the Brotherhood, the penitent bears the sins ; the priests now often have to bear the burden of the sins alone because no one cares ; it is not fair to leave a man all alone in a parish ; if he is in earnest he breaks his heart, if he is not in earnest he is useless. We want to make a living fellowship, an army, and bring in other people to share the happiness we have got here. We must extend the hand of brotherhood. When the fellowship is alive it is splendid. To be a Churchman, a Christian, is still the proudest calling on earth. Go back after your Retreat feeling this fellowship is alive and is splendid. We need more of the spirit, more of the life through the Sacraments, then we shall join with the angels in singing " Holy holy holy, Heaven and earth are full of Thy Glory."

The Epistle for Easter Day

Col. iii, 1-7

First Address

IN this first address we shall only consider this question : What have *you* come for, and what have *I* come for to this Retreat ? And I think the answer can be given in the words of the Bible : " Sir, we would see Jesus." That is what we have come for—to " see " Jesus. All of us at times have thought " If only Jesus were still here and we could see Him, could watch Him with the children and His tender ways with them, then see His expression change when addressing those who wish to keep them away from Him ; watch the shadow and light on His Face ; and yet I wonder whether we should really see Him, or whether we should only see Him with our sensual vision, which we share with all animals, and fail to see Him with our imagination as He really is, with all the truth and beauty and goodness He stands for, see only Jesus, and not Christ. In R. Browning's poem " Death in the Desert " a wonderful description of S. John's death is given, when his friends feel that with his death the last link with Christ will be broken, and S. John sits up and says it is not so. We can, with our imaginative vision, see Jesus more clearly than His contemporaries did. What you see with your sensual vision of other people is only a very small part of them, or what they see of us ; we really know them

88

as we imagine what they are and what they feel : the imagination is the road to reality, the faculty by which we see people and things as they are. A deficient imagination makes people cruel. The cultivation of imagination is the greatest problem, but if undertaken leads to the development of spiritual life. The sensual sight is purely animal ; the imaginative sight is purely human ; the third step, the spiritual insight, finds beauty and truth and goodness in everything, and we must seek for it everywhere. We must gain our vision of beauty and goodness and truth first in Jesus and then we must go out to seek it in the world. Jesus is the ultimate reality of this world ; we see Jesus in the world and the world in Jesus. It is something of what an artist does, he paints ordinary things, fields, sheep, a sunset, but through them he makes you see all the sunsets and their beauty, and if he is a great artist he makes you see all the eternal beauty of truth. Jesus does that for us, but He expresses it in a Life, which is the most lasting material to work upon ; He makes men see in Him beauty, truth, goodness, and it is because He is beauty, truth, goodness, such as has never been reached or surpassed, that He is Divine, and we say He is God. The dogma of His Divinity will and must stand unless we find someone better. To see that clearly, so that it becomes part of ourselves, leads to conversion ; it may come like a flash of lightning or it may come slowly like dawn, but it results in the cry " I see." We must then see Him in others and in ourselves. If we see Him in ourselves it leads us to penitence, and if we are penitent then our conduct towards others will be changed. It is no easy task, but it is a glorious task, and we are here to do a little more of it and to thank God for letting us do it. There are many hindrances to the Vision, but none are such that they cannot be moved.

The best way to meet them is to know that they are there, and to see what is standing between Jesus and us.

(1) *Temperament*.

We have no right to settle down and say it is our temperament, and yet temperament is very difficult to change. In fact, you cannot destroy it, you can only modify it. Temperament is partly bodily ; it has to do with our constitution ; it depends on food, rest, amount of work done, time of going to bed, etc. Therefore there is a bodily side to repentance.

(2) *Disposition*.

We are also born with instincts and impulses which are connected with our interests. Our imaginative sight is largely controlled by our impulses and so we must face them. We must look at ourselves as we are really, otherwise we shall see Jesus through the blurred spectacles of our own selves ; we shall not see Jesus but ourselves in Jesus.

Take the fact of self-assertion which so often spoils and hampers the work of capable, good people. In everything they do they still seek self. Or the contrary fact of a submissive self who shirks work and responsibility through laziness.

(3) *Habit*.

Habit which is accumulated experience and alters the way in which you look at beauty, goodness and truth. Habits are more easily alterable than we think, but we must begin at once and set to work to alter them.

The advantage of a Retreat is the chance offered you to look at yourself and at Him. As you come out of your ordinary life and surroundings and worries, you can, as it were, look at yourself from a distance, survey your own self and then get nearer to Him, and let that view of Him alter your habits.

The Epistle for Easter Day

Second Address

We are taking for the basis of our Meditations the Epistle for Easter Day, but in order to understand it properly we will consider the verses that precede it—Colossians ii, 20 to end.   These verses are extremely difficult; translated freely from the Greek and put into ordinary English they run thus : " If you have in any real sense entered into the significance of His death and have therefore cut yourselves adrift from the empty codes and conventions of the world, why, as though you were still living the worldly life, are you worrying yourselves about these wretched taboos and restrictions ? Things you must not touch, taste or handle.   They are all on the surface and don't go deep enough.   It is all the old business of what is and is not done—man-made laws. Of course they seem reasonable enough as long as you still say within yourself " I have a will of my own and can discipline my own passions and be master in my own house."   But they are all useless as a protection against the boredom and futility of an unregenerate life.   If therefore you have grasped the meaning of Christ's Resurrection seek and keep on seeking that world of ultimate values where Christ assumes His proper place with God at the heart of the great reality.   Think constantly in terms of those ultimate values and not in terms of worldly values.   For your old world is broken and your life centre is now hidden with Christ in God.   As Christ who is your true life centre becomes more and more manifest to you so will your true selves become manifest with all their glorious possibilities. *With this vision as your background* then attack and do to death your merely animal nature, your loose living, unclean thinking, perverted passion, evil desire and covetousness which is just idolatry, which causes your alienation from God."

Dr. Moffatt's translation of the Epistles is a great help for understanding them.

If we want to see Jesus we must enter into the mystery of His Cross; the Cross is the centre of our Vision. It was when Christian came to the Cross that his burden rolled off. It is always thus, either the burden is fastened more securely or it rolls off at the sight of the Cross. It has been said by a very clever man that we have recovered something that the writers of the Creed had lost—we have recovered the living Jesus. It is said that the glory of His Life was left out of the Creed, the beautiful balance of His Life, the clarity of His mind, as both Creeds pass from His Birth to His Death. But it is not true to say so, as although His Life does not come into the Creeds, yet the makers of the Creed had not lost sight of it. All the writers who deal with the historical Christ and want to depict Him as the natural Jesus leave one unsatisfied, as Renan does in his Life of Jesus. They miss out something which is the very personality of Jesus; He was not and never could be only a natural Jesus. For one thing He never shows any sign of being sorry for sin or for anything He has done, and nothing could be more unnatural, but it fits in absolutely with what He says of Himself: "I am the truth and the life." "I am the good shepherd." "If any man will save his life let him take up his cross and follow me," etc. And yet that is the same Jesus who played with children, and was absolutely humble and allowed Himself to be put to death.

Jesus is the origin and meaning of life, yet the search for the historical Jesus has done much good and helped us much. It has cured us of the belief that we can save ourselves if only we follow His example; that we can rise by our own will; that by repeating formulas we can accomplish many things.

All this is quite good in its way, but there must be much behind it, otherwise it leads nowhere.

Even religion may consist of a round of feasts and very mild fasts, going to Communion twice a week, using Duplex envelopes, etc. All these are no real protection against boredom. We make Christ so small that we sometimes wonder whether the Christ of our Churches is the real Christ. We try the feat of lifting ourselves up by our own boot laces. The historical Christ as depicted by writers is to save me by an example. We need example, but we must go much deeper. The question arises : How is it that such a charming person as Jesus aroused so much hatred? What is the secret of His death? He was not an ascetic like John the Baptist, He went to feasts or weddings when He was asked, and He did not sit in a corner mourning over the world's wickedness, but was as an ordinary guest. He was not an Elijah with a sword in His hand. He was not a Jeremiah weeping many tears : He was not melancholy. No, He was very attractive up to a point, but then people came on something hard, adamantine, and they turned round on Him and said He was mad. His Mother said He was beside Himself, His brethren too. And yet He was splendidly sane and sanifying. He was equal with God and gave Himself up to a life of Service. However, those around Him found Him so different they described Him as mad, which comes nearer the truth than saying He was just a natural man. If that is madness, God grant me a like madness. The truth is that He lived in a different world, with a different centre, and when His world came into contact with the ordinary world they bumped together. What is our world? We cannot comprehend the whole world; it is too vast or too minute, so we build a world of our own out of the things that we select to attend to. We cannot and do not attend to everything, so we must always choose, and we choose those things that interest us as they appeal to our impulses; then life becomes quite bearable. But when our world, which is quite out of proportion, bumps on the other world, bumps against it hard, it is entirely shattered and we are broken-hearted.

There are books we feel it is our duty to read, but there are others which grip us, interest us, appeal to our impulses; we live in their world. Those books have any of the following ideas: sense, love, intrigue, luxury, great power, or utter, complete sacrifice; many of the novels are a kind of drug, they make us live in their world. When a little servant girl loves reading about Lord and Lady Cosgrave, it is because for the time she is Lady Cosgrave, lives in luxury, orders her servants about, etc. All novels, like all plays, are not like that. There are plays and novels very different. Bernard Shaw's " *S. Joan* " is one of them; he makes you think deeply as to what is behind it all. We build a world where we are always the hero, or heroine; not only do little people do that, but great men equally. When we find that we do not hold the centre of the stage and that our world is falling to pieces because it is a false world, our heart breaks, and the greater the man is the more awful is the break. Take Napoleon, with all his dreams of a world conquest and empire, and finally his fall and exile at St. Helena, a picture of an utter failure. He was vulgar throughout because he was entirely self-centred. When we are self-centred we only see things and people as related to ourselves; we are the hero, all the other people have only walking-on parts, and the more self-centred we are the more unreal our world is, as we are never heroes or heroines but only just ordinary common or garden people.

As soon as Jesus, who belonged to the real world, came against the little worlds He put His fist against them and smashed them, sometimes violently, as in the case of those play actors the Pharisees ; other times, as with Nicodemus, more gently, and so made him have a glimpse of the real world and Nicodemus departed from Jesus a wiser and a sadder man.

S. Peter, too, was self-centred ; he thought he would do great things for his Lord ; he would stand by Him when all the others left Him, and yet he fell and broke his heart. But that is what Jesus needs. The sacrifice of God is a broken heart. That's why Jesus was brought to His death, as either Jesus' world or the Jews' world must go. And we are all bound to come to that point sooner or later. We cannot live without dreams, and when they are destroyed there is nothing left to live for and we break our hearts. That is the first step, and then we must find another centre—Jesus, not us ; that is real penitence ; the breaking of our heart and world, not in a sentimental way, it is too painful to be sentimental, and making a new world for us with Jesus as its centre. Sometimes instead of shedding tears when we are broken-hearted we just laugh at ourselves, and our repentance may be just as true and sincere.

Third Address

We have seen that the depiction of the historical Christ by so many writers has done a great deal of good, as we have gained much more knowledge of Him, but being only human it has failed to show us

His whole personality. In art also, the picture of the Temptation, which shows us in the forefront Christ as a lonely figure thinking over the problem of His Work, shows us a truer picture than when the devil is very much to the fore. The real world is that in which Jesus lives, and in which He died on the Cross. We all try to escape the Cross ; we protect ourselves against having to pay ; we do anything to avoid the Cross. There are several, in fact many methods ; the following are a few of them :—

(1) *That of the Pharisee.*

We judge others so that we avoid being judged ourselves ; we cannot bear the humiliation of being judged.

(2) *Cynic.*

More common to men than to women. The cynic coats himself round by saying all the world is a bad place and all people are bad ; so is he ; but he is superior to other people in that he knows he is bad and does not pretend.

(3) *Pietist.*

More common to women ; they wrap themselves in a beautiful atmosphere, try to ignore sin, or if they do not ignore it say they cannot do anything for it and it was not meant for them to see it.

(4) *Tyrant.*

He wants to alter the world, but he wants to conform it to his mind ; he works very hard, but after much bustle leaves things just about where they were, as he has not altered the men ; he says there is nobody else to do the work, but really thinks that he is the only one able to do the work well, the others muddle it so very much and he won't let them do it.

(5) *Indifferent.*

That is a very common cause; nothing interests him, so he takes no notice and pretends the Cross is not there.

These are all defences against the Cross. Now Jesus made His Cross both the splendour of God and the sin of man; He took the whole world with all its sin into His Heart. There is something tragic, awful, in that bearing the sin of the whole world; living in, fighting a constant battle against sin, not rising superior to sin but making it His very own, repenting of it, having no self-pity, no pride. We say truly we could not do it, it would drive us mad—and so it would if we were left alone to do it. We are getting very much nearer now to Jesus than when we thought of Him as a natural man. A German writer tried to show that God was capricious; it is a clever book, but written at a time when Germany had an entirely distorted vision of God. We must have a reliable God, and Jesus is entirely reliable; I could never be afraid of what God would do to me; He would not do anything against me. We contemplate Him crowned with thorns, with the soldiers' spittle running down His face, beaten, bruised, and yet without any trace of anger or resentment, and we see in Him the ultimate Glory of God. It seems quite an impossible fact, and yet it is the very centre of Christianity. It always means sorrow and torture and would drive us mad by itself, but there is something else behind it, the Love of God who bears it all for us. That Love, the end, the final, last thing; that burning desire for the perfection of mankind, the full sin-bearing; that is Christianity. The vision of that brings you to penance; the real world as it is in Jesus makes us want to love men with whom we are living although they want to destroy Jesus and His world. So we repent and we come to see the unreality of convention and religious routine. It is no good going to the Sacrament without love for the other Communicants, and with bitterness or hatred in our hearts. But we are not asked to do it by ourselves. Good Friday would be impossible to bear without Easter Day. Death is not the end, but we pass from death to the joy of the resurrection.

Fourth Address

We have seen that we are terrified at having to bear the Cross, but sooner or later it comes to us. Jesus' means of communication with God were not different from ours, He built up His world for Himself, as we do our own, but His was the real world; it was of real value and had a meaning. Let us look at the world He made and see it as He saw it.

He was first of all convinced that it was a *Living World*, with a purpose of its own; that it was no use to make the world fit you, you must fit it. He was a most intense realist; He hated sham. He saw the vision of God in the flowers and the birds and all nature. We think of the world as a dead thing, and try to make it obey our purpose, and find it impossible; it is sheer waste of time. He referred all the time to God's Will, and was perfectly obedient. "My meat is to do the will of my Father." We find that obedience to the will of God as expressed in nature was what He knew, and that must be our first lesson; we have to find the purpose of the world, then fit into it and conform to it.

(2) It is a *reasonable world*, with a purpose that we can find out and comprehend, and laws that we can utilise. But instead of using our knowledge for the benefit of

mankind we use it for its destruction and for evil deeds. In co-operation with God lies our own peace, not in defiance of His laws.

(3) The *world is a gift*, therefore we must take it with gratitude and thanksgiving, nothing is our own, so if it is taken back from us, we only surrender what is not ours except for a time ; we have no right to anything, all blessings are given by God. This was a basic principle of Jesus' world, and therefore the Eucharist is the centre of Christianity. He went further and said that the purpose of the world was the purpose of a Father, a home, a family including all the human family. Therefore we are bound by a twofold tie of gratitude to God and to each other ; we must be in constant communion with the Father, giving continual thanks, and feeling entirely dependent on Him and on our brethren. We owe everything we have, so we must acknowledge our dependence. Sin is really a rebellion against God and therefore a failure of love. The principle of the Fatherhood of God and the Brotherhood of man must be at the base of our conception of the world.

Then finally the world is a *just world*. We must be careful about this statement as it does not mean that we are all alike or equal, but that it is a world where persons are ends in themselves ; not where masses count but where " ones " count. Therefore Jesus held that it is the supreme sin to make men serve your ends, or means to an end. Persons must not be sacrificed to anything ; they are all of supreme and equal value to God. Jesus could easily have dominated His world, and forced it to His way, and carried on His work instead of letting others bungle over it ; but He let them go on so as not to violate their personality— anything is better than destroying people. These are the foundations of His world, constructed out of things as they are, the result of His thirty years' life and toil. These sound like truisms and they are, and it becomes plainer every day that the world cannot be used in any other way; it becomes plainer that if we will not follow Jesus' way we shall suffer and suffer, and in the end be compelled to be obedient. The reason of our rebelling is partly fear and partly pride. It is a difficult way to tread and we hate the Cross.

We may have doubts and wonder whether His way was the right way, or is there a truer one. He bared His breast to the foes and died in consequence, and on Good Friday it looked like the end of all things, but Christianity does not take His death as the end. Which was right, Jesus or His crucifiers? That is the crucial point. We are asked to stake our life on the principle of love and discard class hatred and warfare. Is it possible? It would not be if we were left to do it by ourselves, but we are not. God is on our side, so there is no impossibility. The disciples realised that, as they went forth with triumph, not as failures.

Fifth Address

We see what Jesus' real world was, it meant death and crucifixion, the bearing the sin of the beloved. If that is the real world, can I live in it? That is the whole significance of the Incarnation. The Incarnation is a creative, redemptive act; it means a creative process. God both creates and redeems. God so loved the world that He gave His only Son that whosoever believes in Him should have everlasting life. That eternal life does not mean the extension of this life but life with Jesus Christ. God is for ever seeking us, He is the living energy of creation, of beauty, goodness and truth, always seeking them everywhere. The love of God is the ultimate reality, this becomes in Christians part of the environment to which they can respond. If God had ceased to create, to operate for one moment, the stars would fall out of heaven; if He ceased to be a stimulus there would be no hope, we would in fact go mad. That is what terrified the disciples on Good Friday; they thought all was over, that it had only been a lovely dream. That is what the disciples on the way to Emmaus said to each other. We thought He would have risen. The man who asked me in hospital: What is God like? and when I pointed to the Crucifix, said " That is only one more foul murder, it does not explain the other," and it is quite true if it were not for the Resurrection. The Christian religion is based on the Resurrection. Love and justice are at the very heart of it, they are the very centre of religion. What Jesus succeeded in doing was to take the disciples and in three days to build the whole thing again with new beauty, new energy, and send them out to live the same kind of life, with the same kind of love as He did. St. Francis is a typical example, as his life can only be explained by Jesus' life; it could not have been inspired by any other life. The history of Europe is an enigma unless some solution is found through the Resurrection. The miracle is not only the rising of the body; as the risen body is very different from what it was before, it could appear and disappear, it was therefore not a material body. But He convinced His disciples that He had risen indeed, that He was still operating. It is only by His Grace that we become convinced of Jesus' world and are able to live in it. That Grace is the life that He brought into the world, and it will enable us to follow it and share it.

The New Man in Christ

"If ye then are risen with Christ seek those things that are above." That is, if you are convinced that Jesus is right and His world the real world, then you will live in that world and seek those things that are above. You will have much to bear, which you could not bear if you did not believe in the Resurrection. It will be bearable to go through war, to walk through the slums, to know of horrible cruelty of man to brother man if you know there is a Resurrection, but without that knowledge you must draw the protective armour of the Pharisee or cynic around you or go mad—those are the only alternatives.

Sixth Address

Seek, keep on seeking, those things that are above, where Christ sitteth at the right hand of God—seek, keep on seeking the world of Christ. It has been said that a dumb look in an animal is more moving than words of men, but a dumb look in man is higher than the dumb look of an animal. The highest cannot be said or be expressed. We cannot interpret some words in the New Testament on account of failure to find a word. That is so of this passage. It contains such things as the " right hand," " sitting," etc., and the whole metaphor is so mixed, but it grips us, only we are apt not to go into it deeply. " Above " does not refer to space ; there is no space in the spiritual world ; there is no space between you and one you love. " Above " has no time in it either ; it does not refer to a world that awaits you after death. Just as imaginative sight is above sensual sight, and spiritual sight or sense of value above imaginative sight, so " above " is used in that same sense in this passage. Suppose we put a book of Browning's poems into an ignorant man's hand, he only sees a book with his sensual sight; a school-girl may have a clearer idea of its value, but it is left for a poet to see its real value. The world in which Jesus lives, that is the real world; keep on seeking that until you find it. Jesus calls it sometimes the Kingdom of God; His teaching about the Kingdom may be separated into three different but not contradictory strands, they are the same facts looked at from different angles.

(1) It is our apocalypse, a sudden inrush, a flaming out of heaven.

(2) It comes silently with slow growth, gradually.

(3) It is an eternal reality, amongst us now, it has come on you already.

Seek, is the same word as the one used in the parable of the woman seeking for the coin she had lost. The impulse to seek God and His Kingdom is a response to God's power, and you are not left to yourself to find it; He urges you, helps you; you would not be seeking Him if He did not move you to do it. The Kingdom will come to us out of our better knowledge. The world we have made for ourselves and in which we live is largely false, but we will grow out of it as we keep turning to and seeking after the Kingdom. Our difficulties are often due to the world not being what we think it is, but a mere dream. That search for the Kingdom is the search for the eternal Truth, but we only find it as we express it—in our lives. The seeking of God is the turning of the creature to the Kingdom; the dawning and the growing desire to express it in our lives. We must make the universal concrete, the vision is not sufficient, we must live it. " Seek " first expresses the true value of nature. Next to the means of Grace nothing helps us so much to get near God as the power to commune with the world of nature, but there is a temptation to go no further than see its beauty and so not see Christ in it. The first step in looking at nature is to arouse a feeling of gratitude ; we take a rose for granted because we see so many, like a child having so many presents that it does not notice them, and we say he is spoiled. So God spoils us and we are in danger of losing the power that we can attain by letting custom dull our hearts.

The worship of nature goes beyond sentimentality ; our Lord in the New Testament refers continually to nature. It is the same with the relationship with men and women. Most of us are content with comparatively few intimate friends ; they add to the pleasantness of life, but we get rid of all unpleasant people. We do not take sufficient trouble to get to know men, and yet men were meant to be the chief means of grace. Jesus gave us the twofold commandment " Thou shalt love God . . . and thy neighbour." Getting to know men entails much pain and disappointment and we shrink from the Cross. The Kingdom of God consists of masses of people, not few, single people. The truth is, when somebody says something mean or rude to you, you always connect them with that, you forget that you are just like it, but do not like to be identified with the worst that is in you. Our judgments are always lies. If we go below the surface we find every one is both worse and better than we thought. We have gone a long way from what we thought of " things above," as they concern Mrs. Jones who lives next door. Someone said God made the country, man the town and the devil the suburbs. We think that men are cut off from God in a town, so we leave all the problems of employer and employed, industry, etc., out of the Kingdom. And yet S. John says : I saw the new Jerusalem—a city.

The Epistle for Easter Day

In using many things, coal, etc., we have used men and not known it; we paid, and we thought that was enough; that is not seeking the things that are above. We have not thanked for all our gifts, only taken them for granted; that is why our industrial life has gone so wrong. It will bring us great sorrow when we begin to think of things in that way, but we must do it.

All this is summed up in the Blessed Sacrament. He says: I am the truth about bread. We take bread as representing all natural things that we have sacrificed by our misuse of them, and so crucified Him through our misuse, and we offer them to God for His Glory. When a fellowship of Christians takes bread and lifts it out of the plane of use or misuse to a plane of beauty they acknowledge with sorrow that they have misused them and so crucified Him; they then lift it up, and He who is seeking us like we are seeking Him, comes and takes it and He is glorified. Bread for which men have fought each other becomes no longer a thing to separate us but which binds us together. Everything is in the Blessed Sacrament, all gathered together, and we lift It up and plead His great Sacrifice. The objection the Protestants make that God is everywhere so cannot be specially in the Blessed Sacrament is true, and we must be careful to see that there is no gulf between the sanctuary and the street, the Altar and your ordinary life. We do not ponder enough on the Blessed Sacrament, and so we use it as a ceremony instead of a living, life-giving Sacrifice in which we share His Sacrifice and glorify Him.

The New Man in Christ

Seventh Address

" Set your affections on things above." The word
used for affection in the Greek is the same used by our
Lord in His rebuke to Peter : Thou savourest of the
things of this world. It has to do with mind and
thought, not with the heart. It means that if you enter
into the Resurrection you have centred all thoughts on
Him, you are dead to the old world, you must not think
in terms of earth but in terms of ultimate values.

The Christian life is not complex but astonishingly
difficult. We complicate our life when we think in
terms of the earth ; that is what we are tempted to do
about the size of the world. When we say Jesus is God
men answer that it is impossible to think that a man
made that vast universe. It sounds very wise but it is
mixing up size with value. Quality and quantity are
on different levels ; it is like speaking of goodness by
the yard. Jesus reveals the value of God, a value which
must be measured in personality : He wants you to think
always in terms of quality.

When our Lord asks His disciples who men say He is,
Peter jumps to an answer which earns for him com-
mendation from Jesus, but immediately afterwards when
Jesus speaks of His coming suffering Peter repudiates
its possibility, and our Lord rebukes him sharply : Get
thee behind me, Satan. There is no temptation so hard
to withstand as temptation presented to us by a friend.
We always mix up force with power ; our difficulties arise
in great part from that confusion, and we talk in terms
of earth and not in terms of value. The world, so men
say, needs a God with powerful arms to raise us out of
the mess we have got into, and you offer us a God
suffering, crucified. But force will never accomplish
anything ; love can create a family, but force cannot

bring about a unity of personality or family. To talk about power apart from will and purpose is impossible, it does not exist. We must grasp the purpose of God before thinking of His power. Force is not power; it is tearing the world in pieces, and yet achieves nothing. Men are sighing for peace as they have never done before, but God cannot make peace, He cannot force peace upon us, as there is no such thing as forcing peace; only the power of Love can bring peace. Power to dominate others is really a great weakness, a dominant person can force men to do a thing, but cannot get their wills, the men, themselves; force is only external, it does not touch the inner man; persuasion, leading, love are the only strength and power. God is not armed, you cannot gain love with force; we cannot dominate others or ourselves with force. Also when we reckon our riches, gifts, talent, beauty, money, etc., by what we have it is all wrong, we should measure them by what we give, not by what we have. Peter wanted our Lord to rule, to wear a golden crown, but he saw Him crucified wearing a crown of thorns, and the Christian world has found it so sacred that it would recoil with horror if any king or ruler dared now wear a crown of thorns, to us it is the ultimate sign of royalty. So it has to be right through everything. People when they see you think of your office, your position, they are polite to you, take their hats off, but that is only for what you seem to them. If they discovered that a man of really brilliant capacity, with a brilliant career, had been working for his own end, through ambition, they will no longer respect him or look up to him but think of him as mean. You are worth your love for others and God and no more (1 Cor. xiii). It has rotted its way into all our society that we are what we have, not what we give; yet of your riches the ones you will never regret are those that you have given for the benefit of others; money especially requires great care in the giving, as given without a great deal of love it is dangerous.

Let us think of all in terms of ultimate value, and when you get to the bottom of all you will find that gratitude to God is really what we need and must have and that will give us the right proportion, and teach us the right and ultimate value of things.

Eighth Address

"For ye are dead and your life is hid with Christ in God. When Christ, who is our life, shall appear, then shall ye also appear with Him in glory."

This evidently refers to the second coming, but in another sense He is always coming; with this vision then as your background mortify concupiscence and covetousness which is idolatry. The Apostle puts here covetousness or desire of gain, and lust on the same level; the prostitute and the money-grubber. Then having set people free from botheration about conventions He proceeds to lay down a standard of life; what He would say is : The life I am going to map out for you is impossible unless you are seeking continually to centre your life in Christ, in the life of ultimate values. Christian ethics without Christian religion are impossible. The simplest kind of thing, like the brotherhood of man, is impossible to carry out without religion : brotherhood and unity are impossible in our own strength; that is why S. Paul insists that will-worship is no good. And he speaks from experience, he had tried it. He belonged to the strictest sect of Pharisees; the Pharisees were good people; they were the aristocrats of the Jews. S. Paul had been

108

dominant all his life, but when he saw Stephen and witnessed his death, his little world began to crumble down and in defence of his world he became a murderer, persecuting the Christians. He maintains that you live by worship, not by works. We are not born with a will, but with the material for making one. Most men have not got a will, but must make it, manufacture it, build it up. We build our world out of our interests; and our interests are made out of what spontaneously appeals to us, of what appeals to our primitive instincts.

We are born with powerful primitive instincts, and as long as you remain on that level you are on the level of heathen idolatry. Have you ever wondered why the prophets are so dead against idols? It has been assumed that it was because they were images, but this is quite impossible, as images are not only carved or made, you use them in your speech; you would have to stop talking. The prophets loathed idols because they were the images of primitive instincts. The joy in idolatry is the joy of instinctive action, which gives a great thrill of pleasure and an impression of contact with reality. Whenever there is restraint there is pain. When anybody gets in the way of your impulses it produces a feeling of anger. The essence of bad art is that it appeals directly to instinct and impulse; good art, on the other hand, is the hand-maid of God. The commercialism of art has led to our being flooded with sex literature and pictures as they are the things that always sell. Very few plays or books do not appeal to the sex instinct, but Bernard Shaw's play *St Joan* is absolutely free from it. As a rule it would only attract the few, but it is so astoundingly beautiful that it actually calls to the man in the street. It has sometimes been said that this life is natural and you must not repress the natural impulses. This is half lie, half truth. You must not repress them by pretend-

ing that they are not there, and so deceive yourself.
It is a lie that the natural life according to his impulses
is the life for man, it is the life for animals but not for
men. Man has imagination, animals have not. What
makes you reason is a pain in your mind and reason is
the beginning of all knowledge. Impulses do not
satisfy man. There is no paradise for us or for anyone
until we find something into which we can pour all our
impulses and unify them in the mind of Christ. An
animal can follow one impulse after another without any
harm, man cannot ; he seeks to harmonise, unify them,
and does not find satisfaction and joy until he has
reached that unity. So there must be effort, the impulses
must be directed and therefore partly repressed or
rather, suppressed. The difference is that " suppressed " means that you do not recognise them. You
have to take your natural instincts and consecrate them.
  In Christ you find :
  (1) A King to worship.
  (2) His children to love.
  (3) Truth to satisfy your curiosity.
The only way of sublimation of impulse is the way of
worship. It is what you worship that produces what
you are worth ; you have to seek the Vision above all
other things ; one God, big, large enough to satisfy
every part of you.

Ninth Address

  Therefore. That word is nearly the most important
in this verse : the key to human life is the linking of the
highest to the lowest. It is not safe to be fanatical
about anything but Christ ; being a fanatical Protestant
or a fanatical Anglo-Catholic is no good. It is safe to
be a fanatical Christian (and you will never be a bore)

and that is what Christianity means. But it involves pain, so we are not so liable to fall into it. The essence of religion is to make a unity of yourself round the one only God. That is why it is so important your idea of God should be a right one because if your God is not good enough your religion is a dangerous one. Religion is not necessarily a good thing if it has for object an imperfect or bad God. It is through worship of Him, Christ, that we do to death—mortify—our sinful nature. You are not only in Him but He is in you, so put off anger, sulkiness, malice, hard and abusive speaking.

Anger is not an instinct but the result of blocking an instinct. It is impossible to deal by the will with anger at the wrong moment ; we must go deeper into it. Anger is a sign that an instinct in you has found no outlet, so it is with sulkiness. It is closely connected with self-assertion : you want your own way and you court disaster because you do not want to get angry, but you still want your own way. So the only remedy is to surrender yourself to the will of God, and not to want your own way ; say to yourself " I do not care whether I do the work or others, as long as the work gets done." It is a constant self-surrender, and putting aside of bitter feeling, and of sulkiness. Some people pride themselves on saying : " I never sulk, I just flame out and then it is all over." But the flaming out and the relief of saying hard things is no cure ; it only means that next time you will flame out again and do it more and more frequently, every time it becomes easier. Flaring out with bitter words does more harm than you think, it harms both others and yourself. In " *Dear Brutus* " the dream child had lost a dimple because of a hard word spoken to it. Many dimples are lost in this world for the same reason. This refers not to stern speech which is sometimes necessary, but to " blowing off." In the moment of anger the will is no good, you must turn your mind towards something positive, and do something loving.

Malice is the extension of sulkiness ; it is making a formula of your anger and sulkiness. You should turn and glory in the Cross. We say as long as we are in the wrong we are to confess it, but if the others have done the wrong, it would be the limit for me to confess myself in the wrong. But He said : " Father, forgive them, for they know not what they do." That is it : they knew not what they did. You will say it is not always possible for us, but it is more possible than we think. We miss many people because at the first occasion that they do not please us, we fly off and have nothing more to do with them.

Lying is also a result of a blocked instinct. Sometimes we try to get round it and so use deception. Lying is often due to self-assertion ; we hate humiliation and cannot bear to stand less well in the eyes of others. Go down below and see why you lie. Sometimes lying is due to fear, fear of pain. The place to exercise your will is to turn your attention constantly to the world of ultimate values. In all dealings with self or others remember there is a body—a temperament.

Neurosis is a disease of the nerves caused by worrying too much, not living wisely as to sleep, etc. But God is merciful, He understands and we must understand each other.

Psychosis has to do with your way of thinking ; it can be cured by prayer.

Prayer and auto-suggestion. Either for good or evil you are always using formulas, but it depends whether it is a good formula or not. Such formulas used continually by people can hardly be useful.

" Well, I don't know ! I can't help it." " Oh, well —It is very difficult." " I am always like that. That is just like me "—" I say what I think "—people are rather proud of sayings like these, as if you have the right of bruising or hurting other people.

What is your formula ?

Is it Coué's : day by day, etc.? If that applies to the highest it is good, but if the better only applies to tooth-ache it may not be very helpful. Julian of Norwich had for her formula " All shall be well." Much depends on the content of your formula and the habit of your sub-conscious self. Revise your general formula ; take something that has behind it the Vision : " It will be all right " ; " I shall not lack " if it has the Good Shepherd behind it.

Tenth Address

Recapitulation of all the addresses. New definitions of sight :

Sensual sight that just sees the object.

Imaginative sight sees objects in relation to other objects.

Spiritual insight which sees the ultimate value of objects.

Everybody desires the peace of the world. How can we attack all this ghastly division ? In Him and in His Kingdom there are no divisions, and He must overcome them first in us ; He must give us a Vision which makes all divisions absurd. We feel we must have peace, and yet there is so little we can do towards it.

The first thing is to be quite certain that the cleavage in ourselves is destroyed ; then religious divisions must be destroyed. Divisions and difficulties will never be solved by debates, but by men destroying them in themselves.

The New Man in Christ

When we believe in One Holy Catholic Church and Jesus one in all, we reach to what the world calls a mad idea and impossible to realise, yet this madness is to be our very life; in Him all personal values are first. Class hatred, which is growing harsher and harsher, and international divisions must disappear. Remember that there is nothing you have not received, therefore you owe it all. That is where the Cross and the Resurrection come in; you have received all things, you must share them with others, you must suffer for them, so that your Faith may lead you to know that you will overcome in the power of the Resurrection.

The Hymn of Love

1 Corinthians, chap. 13

First Address

I HAVE chosen 1 Corinthians xiii as our subject for this Retreat for two reasons :

(1) It does contain the very soul and centre of religion couched in the most adequate language.

(2) And because there are signs around us that men are taking the circumference of religion for its centre, the body of religion for its soul. There is nothing more melancholy and sadder at present than the reading of our present religious newspapers : the barrenness of their controversies, the saying unwise and unchristian things. There is urgent need to draw aside from controversy, which is the circumference of religion, and return to its soul. Such controversies are at the present time specially bad because of the immense opportunity offered to the Church at present. The world is calling upon the Church to give it what it needs, and it calls for no more and no less than love, that love that S. Paul defines in its length, breadth, height, the love as found in Christ. We want something that will bind men of all conditions in one unity of love. The world clamours for it sometimes with sneers, sometimes with sobs, and it is when you have heard that clamour that you weep bitterly when you contemplate men quarrelling ceaselessly about the A ar or the Blessed Sacrament. It makes you long to go back to a time when you need not take sides.

So it is very suitable for all our sakes to turn to this hymn of love, which is acknowledged to be common ground. There is little intellectual ability required, and no argument needed.

There are two things essentially that real love, the love of which St. Paul writes, is *not* :

(1) It is not passion.

(2) It is not good nature, natural kindliness, although perfect love has its roots in both ; in fact there is no so-called tender emotion that has no root in passion. The love of the mother for the child, of the man for his beloved, are the roots from which spring the love of God. Charity begins at home but does not end there. Passion is not an unclean thing, but it is an incomplete thing, it is the root which is meant to flower into the love of God, its perfect end. Charity is creative and redemptive, it is not a dull, cold thing, it burns, it is red hot, it transfigures the flame of passion.

(3) It is not natural kindliness, but it has its root in it. Good nature promises so much and brings so little, it is shown to all, so long as they do not trespass on our rights and desires, but it is so disappointing, it has no imagination, it is not the love that Christ meant. Real love is not connected with temperament, thank God ; love is not a natural gift but a supernatural one ; it comes by Grace, it is the gift of God, it is God Himself, the very life of God. It is the gift of God, but it must be claimed by man. God wants to give us love, but we must answer, respond, our part must not be passive. That is the great mistake the Protestants made when they said that nothing *we* did was any good.

The purpose of a Retreat is to seek the gift of God. You have not come to learn, and I to teach you about love, but we have all come to get more of it, to come into closer touch with the source of it : God ; to go out of this Retreat more loving than you came in, and that permanently; to go out more loving to a world that needs love tragically, the precise thing it needs; to go out more certain that unless we are more loving, what we do and say is absolutely no help to anyone and does not matter in the least . . . except to God the All-loving.

Second Address

We must not keep this Retreat as a Retreat from the world, a refuge where we shall cease hearing the clamour outside; that would be a sin. The world is knocking at the door of the Church saying " Have you within a remedy for all the evil, have you anything that will unite all men ? " and we must shout back : " We have, we have, the only remedy ; we have the peace of God which passes all understanding." This ought to be at the back of our mind in a Retreat, so that when we go out we may have more sympathy, more understanding, more love, to show that we have been with Jesus. That we may get more love and show it out, that is why we come to a Retreat. Religion may become conventional, and may become mild, it may detract from reality ; it is not supposed to be passionate. And yet in every man there is a savage, a child and a civilised person, and each of us show ourselves in those characters ; we may show the peevishness of a child or allow the savage to show itself, but we must try to be civilised men, and we must develop each of these, not cut them off. It is only in case of dire necessity that we are to mutilate our nature. " If thine eye causes thee to offend pluck it out." We must develop all three so as to culminate in love. Not love from a sense of duty, as that is a terrible performance for both people. God deliver me from being loved from duty. There is nothing of that in the love of God.

The New Man in Christ

The best way to deal with this chapter is to do what your Aunt Jane did with the books she read, read the last chapter first; so in this chapter it is better to read the last verse first as it explains the first; read the chapter backwards. " And now abide these three, faith, hope and charity."

Faith is the foundation on which the whole chapter rests. Faith is the primitive thing and an instinct, it is the instinct of self preservation; it does not reason, it won't be broken by reason, it only takes account of life. It is the rage that makes a wounded wild beast fight for its life, and it makes you fight for your faith; it fights against death for its own life, the highest life it knows. Man has found in life beauty, truth and goodness and he has found them the highest life and they have become part of him, and necessary to him; he says in fact " If I cannot have them I don't want life; life without something higher is a fraud, but I have seen something beyond the lower life and I have a rage for that higher life, so I will willingly die and give up the lower life to have the higher life which I value." Thus self-assertion turns into self-sacrifice.

There is always electricity in the air when religion is discussed because it is so vital. Religion produces art, poetry, and music. Art is the rage to produce at once what the artist knows he will lose if not put down at once, in colour, on paper. Poetry is created by faith; it is a rage to snatch a thought to prevent it dying and to be kept alive for ever and ever. Faith creates music; it is a melody that only sings in the heart, and the musician snatches at it and puts it down on paper so that it should not die.

Religion is the rage to preserve the highest we have seen, truth, beauty and goodness, and save it when it is threatened by death. So, in a certain way, man creates God, the personification of all beauty, truth and goodness. Religion is the longing that what is highest in me should become reality.

When in the Nicene Creed our Lord is described as God of God, Light of Light, Very God of Very God, etc., it is not meant to be an exact scientific language, but it is the wildest lyric poetry, it is a rage to describe perfection, and yet that does not mean it is not true, only that it is an attempt to express the highest. Faith grasps at the highest life; it is like the tentacles of man grabbing at God (as a shell fish grabs at what is round it) at the eternal beauty, goodness and truth, and God loves to be grabbed at. Love is a rage to perpetuate life at its highest, so Faith reaches at the Eternal Life, and so Immortality is the last article of the Creed. Faith is vague and formless until it becomes Hope; Faith is the substance of Hope, its very nature, without which Hope would no longer be Hope but despair. (Watts's picture of "Hope" expresses what I mean.) Faith alone is so vague, so it becomes concrete in Hope; the hope of perpetuating Christ in ourselves and others, the longing to make the "ought" into the "is." When we know what we want, then faith becomes operative in Hope. Faith is the substance of Hope, Hope is the body of Faith; out of those two love is born. It is the rage to perpetuate the beauty, goodness and truth in Christ, to prevent Christ from dying in ourselves, it is a protest against dying. The mystery of love is the mystery of suffering; there is no love without suffering, love must for ever be crucified with Christ, and enter into the fellowship of His suffering. No love exists without suffering; it is marked with the Cross, but a real Cross, not a home-manufactured one owing to our sins, temper, etc. The passion for the perfection of man in God broke Christ's heart. There was a Crucifixion in the heart of men, but there is also a Resurrection in it. Man meets death and fights it, but he won't be conquered by it, and after the Resurrection there is the Spirit of the Ascension when Jesus is to us God of God. It is in the revelation of the reality that the Spirit comes to us. It is when Jesus is God and meets the Father, that they beget the Holy Spirit, which is the whole doctrine of the Trinity. When we are convinced that Jesus' values of things are the real values, His world the real world, that we realise the dogma of the Trinity. Love is the highest fruit of all our religion, it has in it when we suffer Good Friday, it rises in us in the Resurrection, ascends into Heaven in the Ascension and brings us the Spirit in Whitsuntide. If a thing *ought* to be true, then it *is* true, and it has to be made true through my suffering. Love is the rage or passion to live the highest life, and to go on with it until you are dying, and to die calling : " I will not die, I will not die," and so grasp Eternal Life.

Third Address

Love is more objective than passion or good nature, though it contains both, that is God as God *is* Love. There are things that come between God and one's soul, and the first difficulty is the confusing of oneself with one's gift, or lack of gift. (" Though I have all . . . I am nothing," v. 1, 2.) S. Paul alludes here to speech. It is not because you are a good speaker or teacher that you have God ; you are confusing what you have with what you are ; you make life turn round and round yourself, become self-centred, and it is bound to be a lie. When you rely on your gifts to do your work you are like a gong : and, mind you, people like gongs and they crowd round you, and they confuse yourself with your gifts, and they form a wrong estimate of you. The only way to have a right, true estimate of yourself is in the presence of Jesus and His estimate of you is true ; but very often you take other people's estimate of you and that is most untrue. People value you for your gifts and you can appear to do a lot of work with them, but except the real life power, love, come through you, you can do nothing of any value. The lack of gifts is just as mixed up with the true estimate of yourself ; you spend your time wandering round people with talents and enjoying them. There is confusion between yourself as an instrument, a channel of God and your own self. You suppose people do not need you, do not want you so there is no work for you, and you become so convinced of this that you become deaf to a call of God. Also even when people appear not to want you they may be crying for help all the time. People ask for help in the queerest ways, by gibes, jeers at your Christ, insults. They may be longing all the time to know if your Christ can help them ; often you are needed even when people are not clamouring at your door. If you have not the gift of tongues there remains the ministry of prayer for those who would deny that they needed you. So it is with all the gifts—the gift of faith. People differ in vitality ; those that have more may be led to do a lot of work, but it often leads to pride in your work, and it is the quality of the work, the spirit in which it is done, that matters, not the quantity. So we have two great mistakes to avoid :

(*a*) Confusing between ourselves and our gifts.
(*b*) Confusing between ourselves and the estimate other people have of us.

The root of character lies in a prayerful life where we

can estimate ourselves at our just value and avoid pride
or despair, the two great dangers. The greatest help
to us will be prayer and devotion to the Sacraments.
It is in the presence of the Blessed Sacrament that we
know ourselves best and so do not confuse ourselves
with our gifts. The only way to protect yourself from
dying or getting old, or of having nothing to live for
(as the estimate of other people of us will certainly
change, they will say we are not as we used to be) is to
hold to the very things of God, to hold God in His
very Self, His Love, God Himself. So we shall have
immortality, that is life to be preserved for evermore.
That is what is meant by preparing for death, to prepare
to meet God as God made you, not confused with the
gifts He gave you.

Fourth Address

The essence of a wholesome life is to leave it to someone you know can shoulder the whole responsibility.
All forms of pride stand between ourselves and God,
and St. Paul enumerates them. Our gifts are no good
unless they are put at the disposal of God to work His
Will. That means the clarity of vision which separates
you from your gifts and from what people think you are.
" Though I give all my goods to the poor," etc. Here
we must distinguish ourselves from our works. What
should lead to good actions if not charity ? so we feel
inclined to ask. But all kinds of motives make us do
good actions : love of power, love of praise, love of
patronage. Then is the action still good ? It may
contain a grain of charity and is good so far. Have you
got any goods to give to the poor ? Lots of people
need money, but giving them money is a very dangerous
thing, as you do for people what it is intended they

should do for themselves, which harms them. What goods have we to give? Why should there be any poor? Why are there those savage inequalities? The search for fairness in the world is hopeless. Christ identifies Himself with the poor always. He gives to you all you are capable of receiving and the purpose of what you have is that you can give to those who have not; so if you give to them, you work with Him. There is no good having a sentimental love as it does not last. Who does not know the difficulty of working with an irritable man, and yet love does it, for he is one of the poor. Not only are the poor those who lack money, there are many spiritually poor who need help, and we have nothing to give them, if we have not charity.

Then " Though you give your body to be burned it profiteth nothing," refers to the life of Witness. We bear witness from many motives; we can do it from a feeling of pride " I have promised so I must keep to it " ; from a matter of principles—principles are responsible for many sins. We should witness to Christ and not to ourselves. There was a rage of martyrdom in the Church at one time and being a martyr was forbidden. The most wholesome kind of martyrs are those who do not know they are witnesses, who are just gentle and courageous because it is the only natural thing for them to do, being Christians. To witness without charity does not show Christ. You have to lead people on beyond yourself. All children are poor, they want life, and their mother's love if it does not point beyond herself to God is a failure, and will bring much sorrow to the child. But lest we are despondent let us remember that every little bit of love counts, and although we have very mixed motives a little bit of love wins through it all and it tells.

The New Man in Christ

Fifth Address

The difficulty about practising Christian love is the belief that it is easy. All that is nonsense when faced with reality, because there is little of love in anything approaching the way Christ used it and love is the climax not the start; to be a good lover is to be a perfect saint and there is little of this in the world. We assume that because we can behave ordinarily decently to people, that is love, but this is not at all Christ's meaning. People think love comes by nature and can be increased by Brotherhoods and emotional Societies. Patting each other on the back is not love. We find this in Churches when people stop doing work because they are not properly thanked, which shows there is a lack of love round the Altar, which is a dreadful thing. St. Paul's vision of God and the real meaning of the Crucifixion and Resurrection are behind this Chapter on Love. Love is a supernatural gift, born of faith and hope in each of us and in the whole world and when we are like Him, the world will be what He meant it to be, a world of Love. Love is crucified everywhere and Christ crucified can be seen everywhere and yet He has risen to guarantee that love is deathless and is ascended to its perfection. Love has the doctrine of the Trinity behind it. The Father and Son are One, then Love, the Holy Spirit is begotten. We must move on this plane when reading St. Paul's hymn of love, otherwise the chapter becomes nonsense. There is no sentiment about St. Paul's definition of love; all such pretence is burnt up because the essence of it is reality.

The greatest curse of the preaching of Christianity is that people have got it mixed up with idealism; whereas in reality we have to live with fact and truth. Love leads to the distinction between self and gifts and kills pride, whereas sentiment confuses the person with the gifts, being, like pride, blind. The intellect and the feelings cannot be separated, which leads to a confusion of pride with intellect. The head gets muddled when the heart is wrong. We must have a place of silence apart from the world. There must be a distinction between work and self. The work we do is not ours, but if it is good it is His. We mustn't witness to Christ because we are His, but because He is ours, then the witness is real. It is not easy to do this, but we must lead others on to God and goodness if the witness is to be real, with love blazing through. Love is long-suffering and this is the beginning of the task. Our natural disposition is to be repelled when we find jarring notes in other people. We like being and working and living with people with whom intercourse is easy and we call that love. But as soon as there is any jar we are repelled from people and don't want to have anything to do with them, and this divides us up into little circles, and this kind of love is useless. Being long-suffering means taking pains to understand other people and patiently waiting and watching.

The same thing happens between the classes and between people speaking different languages. It is nonsense to say that class is non-existent; it does exist and makes intercourse between people of different classes difficult, and it is only long-suffering love which can make us able to love people of a different class from our own; or people of a different race and colour. You can form an abstract love for black people, but when you live with them you find them most trying with their different vices and virtues and they find us equally trying. Love, if universal, must be of a higher order than anything we have yet attained to and this is not easy.

Difficulties of temperament are no easy thing ; if two people too much alike have to live together, bitter hatred can be generated between them, and this is the most ghastly of all hatred if there is no supernatural love. That is why monogamy can only be carried on sacramentally. It can be surmounted by the love of God.

The word used by S. Paul for long-suffering means kind, actively useful, doing service, seeking to help and to destroy incompatibilities. It is difficult to actively help those who have unlovable traits, such as pride. There is no room in the world for two proud people because there cannot be two centres. Love bids you ask yourself when you bump up against another person of the same kind if the fault is in you, and not to accept merely surface judgment. A person who appears proud may be suffering from the inferiority complex and therefore asserts herself and hits out. Such people are very hard to be kind to and yet when they call for help one must respond. This sort of person might be someone who has risen to a higher social station and we shut our door against her because she makes mistakes. What we ought to do is to break through because she is much to be pitied. If you want to be kind you must be really interested in your fellow men and must be prepared to watch and wait. Another class of people to whom it is difficult to be kind is the ungrateful people and we think we ought to resent it. If God treated us in the same way He would always be angry, for we are never anything but ungrateful.

Ask yourself why ingratitude annoys you. You ought to want to make people grateful to God and not to you. Ingratitude may be due to bitterness or carelessness. Before being unkind you must find out the cause. It is also difficult to be long-suffering with falsity, untrustworthiness. One is tempted to feel sick with people who are false and unreliable, but we must first find out the truth about it. It is also difficult to be long-suffering with the bitter person who is cruel and cynical, but one must find out, if possible, why he is bitter and must remember that if he hurts others, he hurts himself more. Then lastly it is hard to be long-suffering with fools. And yet one must suffer fools gladly and not gladly make fools suffer. There are loads of fools in the world and they are maddening to work with : only blank forbearance will answer : one cannot look for the cause. But generally all fools have one point on which they are not fools and this must be looked for and found by long-suffering love. It is unpardonable to make fools suffer, it is loathsome in one who is clever to hit a fool when he is down, as it causes deadly friction. Long-suffering argues a place in your soul to which you can retire and wait in the presence of God and take the person and lay him at God's feet and wait before you act. Out of forbearance come wisdom and gentleness.

Sixth Address

The ever present danger of the spiritual life is despair. As you contemplate the meaning of love and realise how far you fall short of the standard there is a danger of despair and so when you read S. Paul's statements you must recollect that every little bit of love counts. If you allow God even a pinprick in your soul to get through He will come because He is ever seeking us. He doesn't wait for us to come to Him. He employs the same method that we find employed in science, the method of longing and breaking through. You have not got to reach the perfection of love before you can begin. You must not pretend at all to God on either side. You must be candid and matter-of-fact and even then you will feel a worm and you have to face disillusion, remembering that the slightest spark of God within you tells. Oh my God I love Thee, is what you must cling to.

We cannot take the task of loving easily, as the man in the street who has never tried it does. S. Paul says "Love doesn't envy." The word used for envy is the same as for zeal, which shows its meaning. Enthusiasm of love, not self-centred. Enthusiasm is a precious thing, it is the cause of all human progress and is never found in the animals. The note of animals is joy and content, because they are finished, but we are unfinished, and our internal harmony has to be made, and it is made by the power of zeal. Love has no false centre for its enthusiasm. False forms lead to envy, misdirected zeal, and this is tearing the Church at present. People are proud of their particular aspect, of being Catholics or Protestants, and this leads to strife. The only safe cause of enthusiasm is Christ to whom we can dedicate ourselves and in whom we can harmonise. The zeal for God will make us enthusiastically loving. Nothing can be done without enthusiasm in this world ; it burns inside and no one could solve the problems of science without it. All the dirty work of the world must be done by enthusiasm, e.g. sick people nursed, etc. Enthusiasm means being possessed by the true God whose face is revealed in Christ. When you envy others, the enthusiasm of your life becomes self-centred and you hate anyone who stands in your way by getting things you haven't got. Envy is a vicious circle, it goes round and round, living on itself, you are locked in and that is death to the soul.

Love, on the other hand, has a right centre for its burning zeal. When you fix your zeal on anything less than God you will see through it and you will become cynical. Life without enthusiasm is not life at all, but is really the beginning of death. Love doesn't boast or exaggerate and is not elated, it does not pretend. It is by this pretending that we perpetuate illusions ; we flatter our friends in talking of them because we think we share their glory but it is liable to collapse and leave nothing. We do this partly to keep up our own spirits. God ought to do this, not we. It means that we have got to carry God instead of God carrying us. " Is not elated " means not pleased with ourselves and then suddenly plunged down into the depths. The real meaning is that love doesn't blow bubbles like we do. And yet you must have something, and if you haven't got real spiritual life you will blow bubbles and be bitter because they have burst. If you have the love which is God Himself born in your heart you don't need these pretences, such as blowing bubbles.

Ponder over the enthusiasms of men and women at the present time. Such things as crossword puzzles, bridge, horse racing, flying ; it is dreadful to see a man centred on these things. People often clash over some false enthusiasm such as a life of pleasure, which is really blowing yourself up. Pleasure can never lead to happiness, only to tickling. A life of pleasure is just a bubble. After forty, four courses remain to you. You either become a cynic and you are damned progressively ; or you become a saint and are in process of being saved ; or you go mad, or become like a cow—one of these four things.

Seventh Address

Any detailed study of a thing like this chapter on love makes it rather terrible and one does not want to mar the beauty by seeing how little we have responded. Sooner or later there must come to us a sense of our own smallness, but this should be compensated by the sense of the mercy, holiness and great love of God. The fact that He works through us while we are most unworthy and a long way off is the whole idea of justification by faith, i.e. being forgiven for His sake. If you love Jesus when you see Him it means that His beauty dwells in your soul. We see how realist Love is, how it loves the truth and refuses lies. Then S. Paul goes on to say that Love does not behave itself unseemly. The Greek means that it is not " deformed," as applied to cripples. The soul that is possessed by love does not behave as if deformed or diseased but is seemly in its conduct. The person who is unconventional for convention's sake is deformed or diseased. Convention used to be the criterion of sin ; tribal custom is the earliest form of moral law ; this still remains. People are not uncomfortable about slandering their neighbours but would be uncomfortable about wearing an unfashionable dress. Some of our customs are worse than tribal ones. Convention should be observed so far as it makes life more harmonious, but if it clashes with love it should have no weight. St. Paul doesn't mean that, but means harmony and health within.

The ideal of health for the mind is just the same as for the body. Love is the way to live in health, but only as you are turned outward and are serving a Master greater than yourself can your soul move in unity. The passion to claim your own rights leads to unseemly conduct because this is a symptom of deformity within because your world still moves round yourself. Love is not easily provoked or irritated. These are two very searching tests for us. The deformity is a deformity of the whole of us. We blame our nerves for our irrita-

tions. We say " I am on edge." " I am run down,"
etc. There is a danger that nerves may prove like devils
in mediæval times. With doctors, nerves are used to
mean " I'm blessed if I know what it is," and being run
down is the cry for help. Nerves mean something
purely mental and the cure is mental or spiritual, by
getting right with God. But we mustn't be blind to
the fact that we and our bodies are an entity and just as
it is mad to take bromide for a bad temper so it may be
mad to go to Confession for bodily illness. You must
not make your nerves an excuse, but if necessary use
physical means and try to find out the real truth instead
of blaming your nerves. When we say we cannot help
it, it means we don't mean to try. To live in harmony
with love is the only road to complete unity within.
(S. Augustine, " Thou hast made us for Thyself O God
and our hearts are ever unquiet until they find rest in
Thee.") You will be told you are a nervous subject
when it is really vitality. Don't trust doctors when they
say you are run down. When grasping after your own
you are poor. The gentle, easy, courteous manners of
the rich are deceptive, they are caused only by their
having plenty and would break down if they found
themselves in want. The rich are never greedy nor in
a hurry. But if they were on the lower level they
would become vulgarians.

It is just the same with our spiritual life. If we have
found nothing to live for, then we grasp at our own.
It is like a dog with a bone or an old lady and her pride.
Only God can satisfy spiritual emptiness and it is the
same with irritability. If you have a strong hold on God
the small things of life don't matter, but if they are
all you have got your hungry soul snaps, because
there is a deformity inside, the only cure for which is
to find God and surrender yourself to Him and rest in

His peace which produces health, and out of health comes reasonableness. (Rejoice in the Lord always, etc., Philippians). You can only be sweetly reasonable if you have God within. That is why we must attack these things directly. If you have no food you cannot will yourself not to be hungry and it is just the same with the soul. That makes the reality of courtesy which comes out of a heart full of love, realising the bigness of those around them, that they are sons of God redeemed by Him. Good manners, tenderness, kindness, etc., all spring from the riches of God within. And so discourtesy betrays something deformed inside : if you look down on others and snap at the porter who carries your luggage it shows you are empty inside and it grieves the Holy Spirit. We have to be as careful of our manners as of our sins.

Eighth Address

No man or woman begins to live a full life until they realise they live in the presence of something greater, outside and beyond themselves. Self-consciousness truly means that you are standing over against that other than yourself and you cannot be living in truth. Wonder is at the base of true living, and wonder leads to worship and after that the great other than self ; it is yet kin to you, you are one with it. Then you begin to live more completely and realise the kinship between you and nature, that out of nature you came and are part and parcel with it, this brings nearer faith which is self-conscious life (opposed to birds, trees, etc.), reaching out to perfection. With us this reaching out is conscious, i.e. faith, God making a being conscious of Him. You are the whole world expressed at a point and the whole world must be lived in you. The world is behind you in your rage to live at your highest and if you refuse it, you die. Faith is primitive and the road to the highest but there can be no result until faith is concrete in hope—the higher life in Him and that is what I want. Hope is faith in action and it then breaks out into love. The Holy Ghost is born of the Father and the Son, being One in our souls.

To grasp that the world is a new birth of a more glorious order of life is to find your harmony and unity in Christ. There must be a death to the old life and we must take this gladly and go through with it and not shirk, sure that there is joy behind the sorrow : this is a further stage in faith, to grasp Immortality behind death and to see Life as an Ascension. The higher life away and beyond the ordinary life is Love proved by the progress of the last hundred years ; the abolition of time and space, and the world crying out for love. In the inner workings of God we can only grasp that love is at the root, otherwise the world would appear cruel and bewildering. We must have gratitude and not pride, humility, the glory of God, not of self. We must go on loving whatever it costs. Being touchy and irritable are signs of a root disease in your nature. The vulgar rich are poor, because they are ravenously hungry inside, and the only cure is to find food to satisfy them. Hungry people are always rude and that is why life becomes disgusting. We are drifting to an internal fate and we say " I can never alter."

Love thinketh no evil. The word " thinketh " is a puzzling word because later in the same passage it is used for thought against another word for thought. (Thought as a child.) The Greek word means all kinds of thought above feeling, reverie or drift thought, uncontrolled thought, the same as in " Why reason ye within yourselves ? " (Christ to Pharisees.) Love succeeds in purifying reverie, and this is the most important task of spiritual lives. You never cease thinking, even in sleep : the mind is never dead. This comes out in dreams, which are unconscious reverie. This natural thought is what we spend most of our days in unless we are occupied in active thought. Reverie cannot be controlled by the will, because it would be too exhausting to keep up. So you cannot will yourself into love or cheerfulness. The only hope is to reach a condition where reverie runs along love's lines and this can be got by turning direct to God in stated times of prayer and communion with God. If the aim of reverie is not to think of love then it becomes a snare and acts of devotion become ends not means. We must not have our minds in a state of evil reverie which leads to our impulsive actions. Wrong reverie leads to idle words. S. Paul speaks of the process of gradually redeeming our reverie until lifted up to love's height, by continued intercession, by blessing people with children, by being grateful directly to God for all the beauty and goodness you see.

This word also contains more than a hint of rationaliatsion, i.e. inventing reasons for the things we do and say and think, and so justifying ourselves when we have other than love in our heart. We have wasted many hours in justifying ourselves and arguing with ourselves for having behaved in a beastly way. In this way you arrange matters with yourself. Lots of controversy arises from this ; not reasoning, but rationalisation. All controversy without prayer is useless. One should tear up three letters and sleep two nights before writing controversially to the newspapers. Reasonable argument is beautiful but it means checking oneself or one's pride and being humble ; it is the supreme test of moral character.

Out of reverie and rationalisation comes the projection of your faults on to other people. This is done constantly if you are bitter and you say others are the same, and this produces slander and wretchedness. You can gauge a person's own faults from the way they slander their neighbours. There is only one way out of the three things arising out of this text, and that is purifying by constant communing with God and recollection of Him and His presence, and the joy of loving begins when your reverie becomes purified.

Ninth Address

The longer you study this Chapter, the more you find it is an attempt like all great art to express the inexpressible. Human language is too poor an instrument except on the low levels of truth. This hymn of love of S. Paul is perfect as to its poetry, but there was much that St. Paul could never say. He first says what speech and knowledge and sacrifice mean without love and says their worth depends on the presence of love. Then he tries to define love by what it does; it suffers, is kind, it sees to the heart of the truth in a person. Charity does not rejoice in lawlessness but in the truth. Natural people find joy in evil second hand; often a kind of deceiving joy like Puritanism; they display the evil of their mind by discussing shocking sins. This tendency is exploited in these days, e.g. the murders on the Crumbles, when people paid to pass through a room where a woman had been mutilated. This is the brutal result of a thing that only grace can conquer, an unclean joy in evil and in discussing people's sins. Love produces a change so that reading and talking about evil becomes a burden to your soul and you won't even think of evil unless obliged. You become a sin-bearer like Christ was and you feel the pain of disgrace to the human race, which you share. A real prophet loathes denouncing evil, but there are prophets who like it. Sin bearing is a very high calling and you can only stand it by the supernatural grace of love. It comes out in gossiping and slander. But love has no joy in this, it rejoices only in truth. There must be some positive basis of joy in you to bear the burden. When you get to this point you are beginning to love people (the damnable human race) without sentiment. You get to look for the tiny bits of Jesus Christ in everyone.

"Charity bears all things" is difficult to translate; it means really to cover up (Latin tego), to hide. It really means Love puts its finger on its lips and thinks before speaking about anything. Jesus did this on two occasions :

(1) When the harlot came into the house of Simon and threw herself at the feet of Jesus, He said to Simon, "Seest thou this woman?" etc. And then told the story of the two debtors to show there are no *sorts* of women.

(2) When the woman taken in adultery was brought to His notice, Jesus said nothing but wrote on the ground "He that is without sin . . . cast the first stone" and they began to go away. That is Love covering up until it gets at the heart of the truth.

Keep these pictures in mind when you say : "Love beareth all things," i.e. putting your finger to your lips and thinking, then saying something sweetly reasonable and yet firm and strong. If only we can practise it, it makes such a difference in our influence whether we say just what flashes into our minds or whether we think first.

"Love believeth all things" : this sounds terrible because credulity is no part of religion, but that is not the real meaning. The word means " trusteth that there is reason and love in all things." Out of silence comes faith in the totality of things as having at heart both reason and love. That can only come out of pausing and thinking, going deeper and turning back. Our trust in the ultimate reasonableness is a supernatural gift, due to the presence of love. If you lose your confidence that there is the purpose and meaning at the heart of things, life becomes intolerable and impossible ; out of this comes a hope, a definite hope at the heart of the universe ; it means something and this conviction is one of the deepest things of religion. There is order working out to an end and this end is the life of love. There is an order in things and it is a developing, moving order, especially in the physical and chemical realm, and there is a faith which has a hope, fixing on the life we find in Christ.

" Love endures all things." The word for " endure " is translated patience, and so is long suffering, but " endures " is the patience that works and plods at things. Love is a fighter, a reformer, not content with things as they are. " Endures " means " conquers through patience," it is that which overcomes the world. Patience that fights and wears things down until they become expressive of order and love. It stands on the rock and is patience born of faith and hope in presence of love's very self. It has the sense of going on along a road or climbing a hill and never giving up but going steadily at it. There is the description of what love does, it ends as this life, which consists in walking on steadily, will do. There's this much joy in it, that the road gets easier the more faithfully we keep on. The first hills of childhood seem terribly hard and so the troubles of the young are harder than those of the old because the young do not realise that the flat part will come later, it won't be all hills. But patience is its own reward and there is never a moment when we don't need it. The troubles of a child seem quite heart-breaking, e.g. when it tells its first lie and is ostracised by its parents who hear it crying in the next room and cannot go to it. At last we must get our feet firmly set and know that if sorrow comes we will go through it. If we keep close to Love we shall win in the end. The troubles of life are described beautifully by Newman in that verse " So long Thy power hath blessed me," etc. The moor and fen stand for loneliness : the crag is the trouble jutting out in your path, and the torrent is the sea of troubles which come crowding upon us. (It never rains but it pours.) When you've gone on, you can help those who are at the starting point, so you can thank God for your trouble and trial and for having been able to overcome it.

Tenth Address

We now come to S. Paul's grand conclusion, the climax and crown which asserts that Love is the end in itself. Love never falls nor fails nor ceases to operate.

Through a glass : that is a problem. We all must come to the question either felt or formulated " What is the purpose and meaning of life ? " As intelligence grows, people seek an intelligible answer. Even the simplest people feel the question but cannot formulate it. Intellectual trouble is the formulation of trouble that begins with feeling. The feeling of unity gives pleasure. People are angry when they cannot think things out. A mechanic and an ignorant man stand before a motor that has broken down—the ignorant man is irritated because he cannot solve the problem as to why the motor doesn't work. Life is an irritating problem. We've grown because God asks us a question, which is the riddle of all life and the answer is the thing to which we grow. S. Paul's Epistle is full of biology, and modern Science emphasises the looking through a glass. We see deeply through instruments the complexity of this weird world. We know much more than our fathers did; unbelievable things are disclosed by the powers of analysis. The more we know, the more complex the riddle becomes and the more we ask what it all means. Through all the world there runs order and intelligibility—proved by the discoveries about the stars.

All this order helps our religion : science keeps us from getting a petty view of God. Our intelligibility shows we are part of the great whole, so does beauty. Beauty argues kinship because it lies in subtle sympathy between the beholder and the beheld. Science gives an immense sense of the great other than ourselves of which we are part. This brings the question to an active-minded person, "What does it mean ?" The Christian answer has been and is that the secret is to be found in man, the highest form of life, man for whom the world was made. It is the custom to belittle the difference between the animals and man, but our kinship in body and mind is being demonstrated. We have instinct and the animals have intelligence up to a point. This is proved by their habits. There is also an immense gulf between the human being and the animal. We must study man's peculiar gifts in order to solve the riddle and the light then begins to dawn. Have you ever thought of the wonder of (1) words and speech ? It is so common that one doesn't notice the mystery. I, when I speak, move the atmosphere and the waves I set up beat on your ear-drum and agitate the cells of your brain, and by some unknown method these motions in the brain cells become ideas and no one knows why. The connection between the processes is sunk in mystery. There is a change in the brain matter corresponding to every thought going through the mind. The animals have rudimentary speech but man alone can pass on his ideas and thoughts.

(2) The gift of music ; we are the only living creatures who possess this gift. Beethoven, who is deaf, thinks music and melodies and makes signs on paper and another person by reading the signs and putting them on the piano can interpret the melody. This is another great mystery.

(3) Art. Man burnt with the pain in his heart to make beauty and did it with colours. A series of electromagnetic vibrations beat on your eye and can be turned into the same colour which burnt in the artist's brain. This is an impenetrable mystery and yet the purpose running through is evident. It means we are not locked up, we can get out to each other and we can grow in the fulness of life and the purpose of art, etc., is unity.

God is Love, a power able to, and aiming at producing a number of personalities and the richness of life that proceeds therefrom. Man invented script of writing which arose out of art. I can pass down the ages what I think and learn to my fellow men at a great distance, and thus writing is the instrument of love. From writing came printing, which is another wonderful gift of God. And so with steam, electricity, etc., up to broadcasting. Time and space are thereby obliterated. God's world demands Love, the power of making people one, and we have to exercise faith, i.e. we have to grasp at life by seeking to do God's Will, responding to His call which we must answer by faith, but it becomes clearer when Love is revealed, and that is the kind of life we must have. The world is made for love and demands it. We are toiling and working out the problem of the perfection of love and we must learn to live in unity in the human race, bearing each other's burdens and fighting the battle of love. And everything we know proves how right S. Paul is in saying that everything we have here is broken and not complete for us this side of death.

Beauty, truth and goodness are all incomplete. The more you enter into the meaning of love the more you realise that there must be the life beyond. You can only be convinced of the meaning of immortality by learning more of the meaning of love. The hunger for immortality is the result of learning love. We shall never write perfect poetry here, but we long to, and that is the rage for Eternity. There are two kinds of worldliness, other worldliness and this worldliness. People ask me what social problems have to do with the spiritual life. I am concerned about drains because I love the people who have bad ones, and it is the same with wages and money. Money is love because it is the means by which we exchange. That which we have made ourselves with these things will continue, although the things themselves end. How I die depends on how I live, and how I live depends on how I love. Everything is a means of making love and what is used otherwise I must try and reform the use of. I must therefore be bitterly concerned about this world for the reason that I want to make everybody loving, which is what the kingdom is for.

That is why I do not feel dreadful when I come down from singing " Holy, Holy, Holy " to talking of drains. Every work should be a means of making love or the " unity of an infinite number of personalities and the richness of life that flows therefrom." God is the goal of this great life and everything belongs to Him. The deeper I think the more solidly I am convinced that this life is the ante-room to something colossal which we cannot begin to understand. In our allotted span of seventy years of life in this world we just get through our infancy and this world must have some grand conclusion beyond. We must:

(1) Give this world's sorrows and pain their true perspective.

(2) Give the wrongs their true perspective.

This sets both your intellect and thought right. I burn with anger about wrongs but not against people, although I burn to cure things.

This life is only a small fragment of what lies in store and heaven means an eternity of life.

You live when you see a laburnum tree hanging over crimson rhododendrons.

As you grow in love you see the face of Christ in the most twisted person.

Comprehending the Love of God

First Address

WE will have our thoughts during this Retreat on Ephesians iv, but I hope you will all see to it that you read the whole Epistle through, but the fourth chapter seems the climax. The whole Epistle was written by S. Paul in a white heat of enthusiasm, it can be seen in the language, some sentences begun and not finished, the grammar quite defective.

We must first notice the " *Therefore*, I the prisoner of the Lord " ; that " therefore " in S. Paul's Epistles must never be neglected as it always shows how the vision of heaven then takes him down to earth, to live the life of the Heavenly vision. The end of the third chapter, verse 16, is " For this cause . . . fulness of God," and then comes the " Therefore." That is the purpose of his writing the Epistle, and we could not have a better purpose for our Retreat, or a purpose better expressed that " to comprehend the love of God, the height, length and depth of God's love. A life in which there is no time for contemplation of life and its purpose, is no life, it is a gradual death, or as otherwise expressed, " it is not a life but a linger."

We all have to live in a groove, even in a life of continual change; the groove is forced upon us, but we must take care that it is a groove and not a grave, we must see that the groove is not covered up, but open so that we can walk in it, looking at the stars above us. Therefore it is to burst open our groove, to shatter the roof over it, to look straight at the stars that we have come to this Retreat. S. Paul always has the sense of the greatness of life, although lived in little things, the conviction that it must be a supernatural life lived in communion with God, by grace and prayer. It would be a disaster if we supposed that the sense of contemplation is only confined to a Retreat. A Retreat is only a means of grace.

The thing that rings through the Epistle is the feeling of the immensity of life and its possibilities. S. Paul always looks at life as a big thing which has a meaning and a purpose. He feels he is free because he has been taken captive by Christ. He was certainly in a groove that might be a grave, prisoner in Rome, chained to a soldier, and he did not want to be, he was so eager, so impatient, to do God's work, and yet he felt free as he made a complete act of self-surrender. That is the secret, self-surrender, and it is to renew that surrender that we are here. Self-surrender hurts, therefore we have never completed it, and so we are not happy. And yet we know the way, it is narrow, and there is a Cross at every milestone, and to avoid the Cross we turn down a by-way, and so we make our way, a long tortuous way, instead of a straight narrow way. Let us take one more step now on the road, and give ouselves as prisoners of the Lord, so as to be set perfectly free. We must find what binds us now, whose prisoner we are, and break away.

1. We may be a prisoner of *fear*, afraid of the future, of poverty, of what people say, of death. What is your fear? Face up to it now.

2. Or a prisoner of *pride*, which binds you in the narrow limit of your own little mean soul; bothering

or believing in yourself, self-centred, judging of everything as it affects you.

3. Or a prisoner of *sloth*, which is the root of all sin, making yourself the servant of your body. Is it true to say you are bone-lazy?

Or you may be mentally lazy, being a busybody, always doing things, so excusing yourself by being bodily active.

Or you may be spiritually lazy.

Second Address

The ordinary secular life of working and resting, etc., becomes a prison without any sense of the supernatural, it depends on His taking hold of us far more than on our taking hold of Him. In moments of doubt let us cling fast to this; He will not rest until we come back to Him and make a complete surrender and give up all idea of any freedom apart from Him. Slavery to Him is real freedom. Let us complete our surrender by finding out what holds us back from Christ. S. Paul bids us walk worthy of the call and when saying this he goes back to his conversion, that wonderful experience related in the Acts. All down the ages there are people to whom Christ comes in this kind of experience, and it alters their whole being, this one subtle, clear, definite experience. S. Paul comes back again and again to the experience of his conversion; we find it in his speeches, sometimes mentioned with joy and sometimes with sorrow. Few of us have had one great experience, most have had many calls—an accumulation of experiences which may be trivial in themselves. We may become conscious of God for a moment, but those who never have these supreme moments, are dead indeed. God never ceases to call, but we only attend spasmodically because we have so many other calls to attend to; it may be in a hymn, or in someone we love, or a good communion, or a simple prayer. Then it all clouds over and we go back and the temptation comes, to think the vision is only a dream, and the whole salvation of the soul depends on our being certain that the running round and chasing ourselves in darkness is not light nor life.

Life is more like Beethoven's Fifth Sonata than the *Daily Mail*. Life is more like a Retreat, a Communion, Art or Love. Then comes the difficulty. If you have that, you get greedy for God and you get impatient of the daily round and want always the face of Jesus Christ, always the thrill, and that means you are not certain about the reality of the vision. The back of religion is that people are grabbing at God because they are avid after their own happiness; they only go to Church for the clear vision of God in the sermon; they won't do work that doesn't bring the vision. Religion must bring them happiness which never comes. You cannot get hold of God for yourself, you must be finding happiness in doing the service of God. We must learn to walk to heaven, not to fly. Patience with real love behind it does find absurdities and complexities in this life. The reconciliation with love's contradictions is to be found in humour.

Cynicism is the surrender to the secular, humorous patience is the reverse of cynicism. There is to-day a belief in secular vocation, that is vocation without God; it is believed that God is not necessary because prayer and communion are not essential, but secular vocation is a ghastly disappointment. Everyone wants a job as a substitute for Jesus, it is a kind of using work as a drug, and it very rarely succeeds as such work is never the best and never gives complete satisfaction. There

146

is a psychology of vocation which is finding one supreme and dominating interest and sublimating the inner nature of man. Souls cannot be saved by work alone, though work may make one forget, but there is no sublimation apart from God, because you are not building a world round God. As the living Christ comes into your soul, then you can walk in a vocation worthy of your soul. We can all find our vocations in Him when we are willing to make the complete surrender. Try to make sure that life is the wrong way up, that the sacred is real and the secular a dream. So long as I do God's Will, I care for nothing ; a Christian ought not to care what happens if He is serving God. We mustn't be greedy of God, we must try and get clear that Christ is the reality and all this going round and round is a dream, and our job must not be refuge from God, but consecrated in Him.

Third Address

There are two sides to what one prays a Retreat may do for you : God's part and yours, the Call and the Response, and there is no doubt that it is the failure of our response which is solely responsible for the failure of our Retreat, as God is always endeavouring and striving, and suffering to do everything for us ; and it is only as we can make a perfect surrender that He is able to bestow on us all the blessings He wishes us to have. So it ought to be our pride, as it was S. Paul's, that we are the prisoners of the Lord, and that we have been made captive by Christ. To see the Vision more clearly and that we may walk worthy of our vocation have we come to this Retreat. Let us then make it our first duty to examine ourselves, and to see whose prisoner we are, and what prevents us from being the prisoner of

the Lord.   And to do that we must get a clearer vision
of God.   We must be perfectly clear and certain that
this world is not the real world, that it is not the true
world.   And yet we are so surrounded by it and so living
in it, that its power is the influence of suggestion, and
by degrees it tends to become a second nature.   But
truth does not rest on suggestion, and a lie, however
often repeated, does not become truth.   This Retreat is
given us to get behind the continual repetition of this
lie, that this world is the only real world.   To " walk
worthy " means to walk steadily in our groove, not
being greedy of God.   We often think God's great and
first duty is to keep us happy.   But there will come lean
times, and when they come, we must walk in the strength
of the times when God showered untold blessings
on us.

Then S. Paul goes on saying " in all *lowliness* and
meekness."   These words to us sound the same, but two
Greek words are used for them, the first referring to
our attitude towards God, the second to our attitude
towards man.

The first is an attitude of humility, a deep-seated
conviction that the world belongs to God, that we
belong to Him, and not that God belongs to us, it means
complete self-surrender, a passionate desire to work
God's Will, not our own ; to use everything not for
ourselves, but for God's purpose.   The great blasphemy
towards the world is that it was made for man.   Blessings are turned to curses when you try to use them
for yourself instead of God's purpose.

Christians are not required to do what the Ascetics
did, they thought that the blessings poured on man
were traps set by God, so they repressed their desires,
which is always bad.   It is not repression that is wanted,
but detachment.   This humility and lowliness is what

148

prevents vulgarity and produces real refinement. It prevents excess of every kind, as it teaches us to use things gently, because they are God's gifts.

Then *Meekness*, as our attitude towards people. It is astonishing how long we can live amongst people without seeing them. We are aware of them as far as they touch us, and we make use of them, but we fail to recognise them as the sons of God, precious in themselves. Nine-tenths of social intercourse is carried on without realising men as they are, or loving them. We think of some, as " to-be-helped people " on whom we make our experiments, a kind of gymnasium of our souls. But you cannot help men in that way. Even friends we only see in their relation to us, not as they are in themselves. This is the root of all class war. If you love people clear-sightedly you must expect to be hurt, and they will be hurt by you, as there is no love without pain. But we must not shrink from that as we do from the Cross wherever we meet it, and go down a by-way so as to avoid it.

Fourth Address

One of the most difficult controversies that has torn the body of Christ in pieces is that of the doctrine of Faith and works. It is at once the oldest and the most modern ; it was always felt that the whole act of salvation was due to God and nothing to man ; that was during the great days ; then came the belief that man is God's fellow worker and finally the belief that man saves himself by his own will, and when this is rife man's worship is at its lowest ebb.

The doctrine that both men and God act is right, but it is quite plain that good works need not be saving things either to the doer of them or to the object to which the works are done. It is quite clear that what makes them good is what lies in the personality of the person who does them. It might seem that what S. Paul asks is elementary, viz. to be meek in our attitude to our fellow men, to be humble in our attitude to God and the Universe and to put up with one another in love; but what underlies it all is the fact that there are many kinds of patience, meekness and humility, and the power of these virtues, S. Paul says, will be proportionate to the brightness of the vision, for the aim is immense, viz. love, but the means are quite ordinary. To become a great lover means that through you is shown the redeeming power of the world and you are the ambassador of God, and in proportion as you have laid hold on the vision of God, you become a channel by which the whole of God's spirit is permeated into the world. We know there are different kinds of patience, etc., some of which redeems and some of which hurts, and the outward manifestation may be the same but the spirit different.

Then you have a sense of immense possibilities in ordinary actions, e.g. the boy at Rugby who said that the greatest influence in his life had been Bishop Westcott, and yet he had only heard Westcott preach one sermon, he had had his Greek prose corrected by him and had been taught Latin by him, all of which shows that behind Westcott there must have been burning the fire of a great vision. S. Paul believed in vision but he sees that conduct is the sacrament of spirit. Is this practical in our ordinary dealings with our fellow men? Can we suffer fools gladly for Christ's sake and put up with the faults of people with whom we live? It is the only way if done on a high level. One must develop a habit to pray about someone on the spot, that is the real secret of influence. The danger of religion is that things like formal times of prayer and the externals of religion tend to become a chain if we are not on the look out. If the real presence in the Sacrament doesn't lead to the real seeing of Jesus in the world it will become a curse and not a blessing. The secret of influence is to pray for people deliberately. Out of weakly, unreliable, proud people, etc., the tragedy of the world is built, but out of the same kind of people, Christ, by over-coming the things that make us ridiculous builds His Kingdom. Out of ordinary patience raised to the highest level is being built the Kingdom of heaven. We must have the power of being alone with God when with others, especially when irritating and brutal things are said we must be capable of offering it to God and giving the right reply. This is not impossible although difficult, and it is worth while going on and persevering in it.

Fifth Address

We have set ourselves this Retreat to work out for ourselves the deeper implications called forth by the idea of vocation. We have found that there is always a link between heaven and earth, and that is what we pray for when we say " Thy Kingdom come—on earth as it is in heaven." We have many ideals and a Vision, but unless we work them out in everyday life they are lost and vain. Just as we may have many beautiful ideas, but unless we go through the travail of putting them into words, the poem does not exist. We feel keenly the difficulty of reconciling all the complexity of our life with the Vision we have, and working out the Vision into our daily life. We have come here apart that we may see the Vision more clearly, and that we may be more ready to see the Sacrifice and the Cross in front of us, and learn to walk along the narrow way, and not round the Cross to avoid it if possible. The only thing that will help us is being made captive by Christ, His prisoner, and to walk steadily in the groove God has appointed for us, not the grave dug by ourselves. And if it appears that the fruits S. Paul speaks of are simple and rather a low ideal, we must remember that the worth of works lies in the spirit in which they are done. Humility, it has been said, is the most uproarious of virtues as it sets us so completely free from everything, even from the greed of God. It is a positive virtue when carried out in the proper spirit, and the same is true of meekness, patience and forbearance.

But remember it is no easy task to love God and your neighbour too. The more you love God, the more repulsive will become your sins and those of your fellow men. And the more you try to love men goodnaturedly, the less you will see God in them. Then S. Paul goes on "Endeavouring to keep the unity of the Spirit in the bond of peace." That word used, "endeavouring," is a very strong Greek word, used to apply to the work of the galley-slave that brings sweat on his brow. That is the task that Christianity sets us, in the interweaving of love of God and man. Christ calls us to this tremendous effort of keeping the unity of Spirit in the bond of peace. Perfect unity, we feel, is an end in itself, as it means love which certainly is an end in itself. When we are with a friend or someone we love deeply, we are quite satisfied, and we no longer ask, why we live or why we were born. We feel we were born for this. But it is difficult to attain to this unity of love with a number of people round us.

The first unity of love is the *home*. Here we feel it must inevitably be heaven, as one takes it for granted that members of a family will love each other. And yet it is not so, as if there is not something more than natural love between husband and wife, or father and child, the love will not stand. And in fact no one can be so intensely detested as a relation. The thing is that they idolise one another, so naturally the love is bound to dissolve. We must keep in sight the unity of the Spirit, as otherwise we shall try to dominate, turn our love into a possessive love, or what the Church calls it, an inordinate affection.

So in *friendship* we have to strive constantly to maintain the unity of Spirit, feeling that our love is built on that foundation alone, with God uniting us in love to Him.

Then there is Unity of *work*. Work ought to be the happiest relation between fellow workers. That is the tragedy of the working men at present, that there is no unity of spirit in their work, so when they are set free to play, there is no unity in their play and so it is useless. When we are joined together as workers, whatever the work may be, there is a terrible lack of unity of spirit, and it is specially dreadful among workers round the Altar, as that ought to be the highest work, and it is continually spoilt by jealousy, pride, ambition, hatred. It makes this lack of unity all the worse by contrast to the Altar, and what the Altar means. If the simplicity of Christ in the Sacrament cannot subdue these feelings of jealousy, ambition, hatred, nothing can, but the Sacrament can.

Then there is the Unity of nations, in which the same rule applies. Without prayer and Communion, and the simple faith in the love of God, all our unities are constantly broken by hatreds, pride, etc. So these apparently simple things, humility, meekness, forbearance, patience, demand effort, but not hopeless effort, as behind all our divisions we are really all at one; only let us clear all away and return to the simplicity of the Eucharist and its clear teaching. There ought to be no possibility of controversy about the Eucharist, there might be conference, but in any case no newspaper is the place for such a controversy, that is sheer blasphemy. There is no schism among the saints, there is only worship.

Sixth Address

S. Paul sees God in the glory of His Eternal Love, and sees once again the Vision he saw on his conversion, and he trails it back in golden glory to the rut or groove. He says " I who am chained, doing what I am compelled to do, knowing that God commanded the light to shine out of darkness, turn to you and say that ye ' walk worthy of your vocation.' " The purpose of the Retreat is to carry the Vision back to our little round of futility. The fruit of the vision of the high standard of patience, meekness, etc., which we set before us, results in a great effort to keep before us the unity of the spirit whether in family, factory, friendship, city or world; try to realise that, only as we are one in God can we be bound unbreakably together. We must not trust the natural affections in any unity whatever. Then S. Paul breaks off (in R.V. " For " is omitted), calling out " One body." The word " Body " in the New Testament is used with three references.

(1) Human body, temple of Christ because temple of Spirit.

(2) Church which is His Body.

(3) Blessed Sacrament, " This is My Body," etc.

Let us think about these three kinds of bodies.

The root metaphor is the physical body, as the other two are drawn from that. The Body of the Church is

related to Christ in the same relation as the human body
is related to the spirit. What *is* the relation between
the human body and the spirit? In many people's
minds they mean just the opposite, the flesh being
the lower part, the spirit the higher. The dualism
within us is thought to be the conflict between the body
and the spirit, but that is a wrong way of looking at it.
The body is the means whereby the spirit expresses itself.
The body is a combination of chemicals, gases in various
forms, it is a most wonderful combination, being the
building up of atoms by life. Life is an active creative
principle which combines the many cells into a com-
plicated machine. This complexity is more and more
revealed as we know more about the body; strange
faults and failings are revealed. The astounding
adaptation of the body is marvellous. The body is not
an end in itself, it is a machine running according to
inviolable laws, it can be oiled, can be taken to pieces
and put together again, can change its chemical com-
position by means of medicine. There are three things
to be observed about the body.

(1) It is initiated by intelligence.

(2) Controlled by the mind.

(3) Adapted to a purpose.

Every machine is governed by these three things. It
took years and years of intelligence to invent a simple
printing machine.

Our bodies are things wrought out for a purpose by
an infinite mind, they are controlled by a mind which
hovers over them, leaving them free but yet directing
them, they are made by God, for a purpose outside
themselves.

This combines the scientific and religious way of
looking at the body, and these two agree. The human
body is made to be the carrier of something other than

itself, i.e. the mind, and is therefore a means to an end
and not an end in itself. No bodily pleasure or sensual
joy is an end in itself; these are permissible but are
not the object of the body. Nor must the body be
treated as an enemy and neglected or abused, but it must
be looked upon as a marvellous carrier of the mind.
The mind is still more amazing, it has mechanical
aspects but is not a machine. Formerly the mind was
a mere consciousness. "Unconscious mind" was a
term invented to show that the mind was bigger than
our consciousness. In the desires the mind and body
meet, because in the animals the passions are a natural
unity, therefore they are born happy and remain happy.
Our passions are not grouped in any natural harmony,
but meet in intelligence and can drag the body down
to die spiritually or to be elevated by God to make both
serve the spirit's purpose. The spirit is that you which
is in the mind of God, your spirit is God's spirit working
in you and producing in you the capacity to grasp the
fact that behind the purpose is a Purposer who is your
Lover and Friend. The struggle lies in the mind which
is either dragged down to the body or lifted up to the
spirit. The spiritual is not the "not bodily" but the
meaning of the mind and body, and the power to grasp
that meaning.

God's supreme achievements in the body are :

(1) Self-conscious individuality which is the basis of
your uniqueness. No two persons' bodies are the same.
We are different from the animals in that we become
unified in the spirit to serve the highest, so the passions
can be lifted up and become the centre of a unified
stable character. This individuality can be reached by
other individuality. My power of reaching you is
through my body. Personal influence is bodily and this
explains temperamental likes and dislikes.

Through the body there comes into birth :—

Love, the second purpose of the body, which is the union of our individuality with another and then is given the power of conceiving God. One may think that this is a purely spiritual process, but with every thought I have and conceive there is a chemical and organic change in my body.

So the three ends of the body are :

(1) The unity of self-consciousness.

(2) The power to enter into self-conscious inter-course with others.

(3) The power to enter into self-conscious unity with God.

These ends cannot be attained completely in this life ; unity with others is only at its beginning, but they will be attained and completed in the Resurrection body, which will realise the accomplishment of all three functions.

As a self-conscious body we shall enter into our risen body.

The idea held by some that our bodies will be absorbed in God, cannot be true as it would argue that there is no resurrection of the body. God the Spirit Himself completes the three functions of the body through His Incarnate Son. If then we are wiped out entirely, the Universe is without a purpose.

The purpose of the body is the purpose of the whole world. It has taken the whole of the Universe to make your body.

Seventh Address

" I bow my knees to God the Father of Our Lord Jesus." This is really the beginning and the end of all things. It is the expression of dependence and the glad acknowledgment of it to God the Father and therefore the root of all religion. One body, one spirit. Think of your body, realise its complexity, its delicacy, and the way it is made to serve its purpose; do not look at its imperfections, those are the scars and the wounds. Think I am a self-conscious individual capable of loving others, and the Universe of God. We are all one Body, and One Spirit, God.

Your body is the simile used. The Universe is one body because the Church is the body of God in Christ, as the Sacrament is the body of Jesus. My body is the expression of the Universe, the whole Universe. Take the sun, which my body needs. But even if I felt the sun continually I should die unless I had food and drink, but when I take nourishment I absorb the sun through vegetables and meat and I live; so my body is the expression of all the universe and the purpose of my body is the purpose of all the world, and is expressed in individuality. It is a vicious way to think of natural and artificial being opposites, as it would shut out God out of towns, which are artificial; let me divide things into what is good and what is evil. We have rendered the world as complex as our bodies, but all discoveries are only extensions of our natural bodies, whether eyes, ears, lips, legs, etc., in television, telephones, motors, etc. The men who invented them did not know what they did, but God knew, and they have built the world into one big, vast body. God's purpose is creating numbers of self-conscious beings, dependent on each other and glad to be so serving each other and being served by them, bound together by a common loyalty and worship to the One God. And it is the hope of your calling to live in the new world, the Church of Christ, the Body of Christ. But just as Christ when He was on the Cross appeared a dead failure, so the Church appeared at Pentecost. To a Roman citizen it appeared no more than a little band of drunken men, shouting and excited. And yet it has come down the ages growing in strength, but still crucified and often ridiculous in its pretensions, and split into sects, its blindness, its everlasting arguments, and yet incomparably the sweetest, cleanest, most wholesome institution of the world. Our contempt of it at times is justified by our belief of what it ought to be in the Divine purpose. I believe in it as I believe in Christ, as it is His body, and our hope is reaching out to what it will be. Our faith in it is a continual battle against the baseless suggestion of the world that it is nothing but a failure, and the spiritual life consists in crying out continually it is One Body, One Spirit.

The basis of your belief in the Church is that the Spirit that created the world is working His purpose in the world through the Church. The Church is the unity of self-conscious free men, so there can be no persecution in the Church, but only a high standard of tolerance. The Church is the union of free men bound together by a common vision of God, and the Church is to realise the three purposes.

Then there is the Body of Christ in the Blessed Sacrament. What is the relation between the matter and the Spirit? Which is the bread and which our Lord's body? The relation is the same as between our body and our spirit. The relation is certain, but we have no knowledge, and cannot have, how Christ is related to the bread, but we know He is present in the bread, Christ takes the bread and uses it as His Body, to come as a self-conscious body to another self-conscious body, by which means He comes to me, and thank God, I come to Him, and we are One, One Body and One Spirit, Jesus the foundation stone. If we could order our minds on that belief it would help us very much.

The Sacrament is nothing but Christ, like my body it is nothing, and yet it is everything; the element is nothing; but Christ is everything. We can say with all Protestants that the bread is still bread after the Consecration, but to say it is *only* bread is sheer madness and nonsense as it brings us Jesus in our Communion.

Eighth Address

" The light shines in the darkness and the darkness has never swallowed it up." In this passage the darkness appears from nowhere, no account of its origin and purpose can be given. The problem of evil lies athwart all life and there is no solution; we have to destroy, not to explain. There is no more exercising problem than that of evil, there is no why about it, but the light has never been swallowed up by the darkness. S. Paul cries out because he has seen the light and because we have to walk in the darkness, he bids us renew our vision and hold it fast that we may walk worthy of our vocation. We must remember there is one body and think of our own body with its threefold achievements. The purpose for which all bodies are made is the same, viz., to create. The Body of the Christian Church is crucified on earth and ever rises again and binds itself round the body of Christ as a unity. " Because there is one Lord, one faith, one baptism," etc.

Faith is just life, all that lives lives by faith. The word " faith " leads rather to confusions between the holding of creeds and dogmas, etc., and looking upon those as ends in themselves to getting to heaven. There is no such thing as the expression of ultimate truth; artists, poets, teachers all know this. Dogmas are at best symbols and more of the nature of poetry than of science. Faith is not primarily a matter of intellect, but it is the climax and crown of the deepest impulse of nature, viz. self preservation, which is life itself or the essence of life. The meanest creature fights for itself, but the impulse is more vivid in animals. This impulse in man undergoes a change as it climbs higher and higher. The lowest faith grasps at life for the body and is selfish though still faith, but it soon changes and men begin to fight for their tribe and country or even against their country for beauty, goodness and truth, e.g. Jeremiah.

The impulse to live grasping the best kind of life and to preserve it, that is faith. If it were not for this impulse to get to a wider life man would never be where he is and there would have been no progress towards civilisation and the Church. Men would never have known God, had it not been for those who couldn't live without Him. We believe in God, because we know we cannot live without Him. The hunger in our heart is best expressed by the words of S. Augustine, " Thou hast made us for Thyself O God and our hearts are ever unquiet until they find rest in Thee." There is only one faith running through the human race and that is grabbing for the highest life, groping after the kingdom of God. The same faith drives a man to drink and to God. But this force does not become operative until it is attached to a hope. Faith becomes incarnate in hope. This groping after a higher life only leads to action when something like Socialism in a man becomes his faith. There is a clamour of hopes and one cannot distinguish between them. S. Paul says there is one faith and one hope to meet it. If a man believes in money, he creates a picture of the world as a place where money can be made, and it is just the same with education, etc. We all make unities of the world. Some intellectuals, and all poets, make pictures of the world and one must find out what picture of the world people are making; the most common one is the struggle for existence. The working class picture the world as a fight between two armies, masters and men. Some men think in sounds or words rather than in pictures. We live by pictures of the world, we can't help it. Some of our pictures are merely personal and we always figure as the heroes because our surrender to God is not complete. We must learn to cease to be the heroes of our own plays, we are much safer as scene shifters.

Men will only fight for faith; all wars are religious. We are all living in these dramas, some big and some small. S. Paul says there is only one hope and that is the picture of Christ. It seems narrow but it is impossible to regard anything as a true interpretation which cannot come into the Christian drama. The meaning of the world is played out in dramatic form in the life of Jesus. The Early Church put its hand on that life and took out four great scenes. The *Birth*, the *Atonement*, the *Resurrection*, the *Ascension*, and these four pictures are the centre of the Creed. It is the Drama of life, and Christ is the Centre. It is the new kind of life being born (Christmas), agonising (Good Friday), triumphing (Easter) and progressing through suffering (Ascension). It all means the new life. The Christian religion has always preached and prayed to those pictures until the world means just that to us, all our devotion, worship, prayer, etc. God speaks to us through these pictures. We were not saved two thousand years ago by the Cross, but we are being saved now. This is the one hope and our faith is safe when attached to it. We must be born again because all life is a response to a call. The Cross goes straight upwards; it is the only thing that does and without it one goes round and round, and only through meeting the power of the Cross can we ever hope to go straight upward. We must find the unity of God through Christ on the Cross. To live in a world which means this is the whole Christian faith, the life which is God centred and man-loving. We are a living Christmas, a living Good Friday, a living Easter and a living Ascension Day, and so is this struggling world one vast Christmas, etc. God shines through these pictures to give the light of His love to our hearts. The Word became flesh, etc. It is the noblest, sublimest, fullest account of life's meaning and to that I pin my faith and out of that comes my love. I believe in love, not force, in faith, not cynicism, and all my devotions are just letting God speak to me through these pictures. The Christian faith is an historical faith.

Philosophers and others make unities and good schemes of the world as far as they go but they don't embrace the whole of it. Nothing is any use but a dramatic picture, which shows the picture in terms of life. There are many people who scorn that faith and say they haven't got it; everybody has a faith only sometimes it is so mean they dare not produce it, most probably they worship only themselves. You cannot knock a faith into anything but a shape that fits the form of Christ, but any form of faith which has ever produced one Christian cannot be ruled out.

Ninth Address

We have seen that if you have renewed your complete self-surrender, that call makes you captives of the Lord Jesus, and if during this Retreat you have made one step forward, you may be satisfied that the Retreat has not been in vain. Remember that God will not forget you, even if you forget Him, He has greater hold of you than you have of Him, and if you make a real effort to walk worthy of your vocation, we have not met in vain. You have pondered on the miracle of your body and have looked on it as a marvellous instrument for realising your individuality and your union with God : and that, the purpose of your body, is the purpose of the world.

Now we come to the next point : " One baptism, one God." These two words bring us with a shock from the highest spiritual level we have been considering to two definite points : cultus and creed. They bring us at once to the doctrine of the Trinity and the rite of Baptism. What relation does this high faith bear to the Unity of dogma and the ritual of practice ? How far as Christians are we compelled to have the dogmas of the Church ? It has always been an agonising struggle. In the play of Bernard Shaw, *S. Joan*, the struggle is well brought out. S. Joan in all she says in setting herself as directly inspired, condemns herself by every word she utters as a member of the Church. What is a Church to do with those who cannot accept ritual or dogma ? There is no solution. I think we must tolerate heretics to the last bearable point, and include in the Church any Creed which has produced even a few Saints.

Yet as to ourselves we must remember that heresy is an enormous responsibility. Authority is the accumulation of the experience of ages, and the authority of the Church cannot be lightly thrown off, and yet one hears often said with a sense of pride, " Oh, I am rather a heretic, you know." The first authority for a child is the authority of parents, and their word is law at first, then they rebel in part and that is a time of acute danger, as they think their parents are no good. In this very dangerous period, nothing but the love that they should have for their parents, can save them. This Creed and Worship we have is the accumulation of ages, and it is right we should keep them and bring our children up in them. Then when difficulties come, we must admit growth and yet we must insist that this experience cannot be altered to suit anybody, and is not lightly to be put aside. It is easy to be heretical and probably wrong and we must act with great care, and with much thought, and we must not expect to have the Creeds changed for us. Then comes the question are we to turn out anybody who does not hold the Church's Creed in its entirety, say who does not hold the Virgin Birth? No, I do not think so. The authority of the Church must be temperate, there is room left in the Church for extremely wide differences, and complete uniformity is not possible.

The same applies to Ritual. How far must we adopt uniformity? Rome is extremely imposing in its absolute uniformity, the English Church is very different, and people say "we never know what to expect." We think it should present a united front to the world, but its real strength is the Unity of Spirit with diversities of ritual. There is a real danger that we shall be tempted to break out in controversy about the ritual. Let us remember that dogma and ritual are means to an end, and not ends in themselves, and if we approach them controversially we are sure to go wrong. There is only one way of showing that our way is right, and that is by proving what fine men it produces; to take a strong consistent line and show forth in our lives that it is a brilliantly clear road to Jesus. Religious controversy is always due to a sin somewhere.

There are some that say " I love Jesus, but I cannot

do with organised Christianity," but if you want to be saved alone, you may not be saved at all. They want to find a Church that will contain their conceit, and it does not exist, the Church exists for all, not for " one." But with all that, this is a very difficult time, but also a glorious time, so keep firm, distinguishing means from end, and above all things have fervent charity.

Finally let us hold before our eyes the saintly lives, and be as near in your life to the life of Jesus.

The Great Commandment

" Thou shalt love the Lord thy God with all thy heart, and with all thy soul, and with all thy strength, and with all thy mind, and thy neighbour as thyself."

WITH this resolution then firmly made let us study ethics in the concrete, and test our progress in the study by the results produced in our own lives by the author of all concrete good, Jesus Christ. He did not come into the world to compose philosophical theories. He came into the world to make good men, and when He was asked what the first and great commandment was, what the secret of all good living was, He replied without hesitation. " Thou shalt love the Lord thy God with all thy heart, with all thy mind, with all thy soul, and with all thy strength." This according to Jesus of Nazareth was the first essential for mental and spiritual health, the love of God. Then after that and depending upon it, the love of one's neighbour.

Now if we take the view of the commandments which brings their truth to the test of results this means that the first practical necessity of human life is to get right with God. This is a conclusion which the world, and more particularly the modern world, tolerates in theory, but in practice continually rejects. From the practical point of view the majority of men in the western world have agreed that we should reverse the order of the commandments which are given by Jesus of Nazareth, and put the second one first. For them the first and

great commandment is, " Thou shalt love thy neighbour
as thyself," and the second is like unto it, but manifestly of secondary importance, being mainly a matter
of temperament, upbringing and taste.

They would say you must love your neighbour as
yourself if you want to be a decent man, and then of
course if you were inclined to be religious and enjoy
listening to sermons and singing hymns, you should
love your God, and not play golf on Sundays. But
don't go too far with this serious business or you will
probably become a burden to yourself and a nuisance to
your neighbours. For heaven's sake let us be broad-
minded and tolerant. It is perhaps a good thing to
believe something, but it does not matter very much
what you believe so long as you are consistent. Religion,
like beer, is a good thing taken in moderation. It
certainly has its uses, especially for women and children.
It may even be good for business. It serves to keep
working people quiet and to prevent strikes. It is, in
fact, like art or music, a beneficial luxury.

This in varying forms and expressed in different ways
with more or less honesty is the real attitude of the
Western civilised world to religion. If it is right,
Christ is plainly wrong, for He did not lay down this
law as a counsel of perfection for saints. He laid it
down as the only hope of sinners, and there is no hope
for compromise between the bland and rather plain
patronage of God which the practical man assumes to
be right and reasonable, and the fierce insistence of
Jesus upon the necessity of complete surrender to God,
continued prayer and communion with the unseen. It
is Christ or the practical man. It is one or the other
for it. Which is right ?

Well, let us look at it a little more closely. Suppose
we leave the first and great commandment out and take

the second as a summary of life's necessity. "Thou shalt love thy neighbour as thyself." "Do unto others as you would they should do unto you." It sounds right, but is it? What do you want them to do unto you? How do you love yourself? Mind you, Jesus never said you were not to love yourself. He was far too wise to ask for impossibilities. But you can love yourself in many ways. There are all sorts of love. How does that mother love her child? Maybe she pampers, pets and coddles it, giving way to its every will. What is the result? The child becomes a nuisance to itself and everybody else. You could love yourself just like that. You can carry a cushion instead of a cross. You can feed, dress and pamper yourself, but suppose you then love your neighbour as yourself.

What good will that do to him but make him as big an ass as you are, and that's about all? Your love will be worth nothing because that is what you are worth. There are lots of good fellows; but there are lots of good fellows whose love I would not take as a gift. They have not anything in them, and so their love is as worthless as their hate. You may love yourself and desire to make yourself rich and powerful, to make yourself prosperous. You may love yourself and want to get on. Then you love your neighbour as yourself. You want to make everybody rich, powerful and prosperous. You are a public-spirited man. You are out for the " god" of your country, your city and even of the world.

A prominent official of the U.S.A. Chamber of Commerce speaking at a dinner, preached this gospel with amazing force and fervour. His subject was the greatness of America, and his argument was simplicity itself. The happiness of life consisteth in what he called its satisfactions, and satisfactions were

in the main material possessions. A civilisation was to
be measured by that standard. A man's life consisteth
in the multitude of things that he possesseth. America
possesses an enormous multitude, an increasing number
of things. Therefore she was great. Her agricultural
produce had gone up from twenty billions of dollars to
seventy-eight billions in ten years despite the fact that
one million people had migrated from the country to
the town. America used to have one telephone to
every fifty people. Now it has one telephone to every
eight. It used to have one automobile to every thirty-
five. Now it has one to every twelve. It has the
highest standard of life in the world.

Go through Europe and you could not find anything
like it anywhere. With a thrill of triumph in his voice
he discussed the amazing growth of American railroads
from a little wooden track somewhere near Boston to
the present vast transcontinental system. It was wonderfully done with a wealth of statistical and technical
knowledge, and there was the glory of power and the
growth of wealth in every word. This was the greatness
of America and her mission was to raise the world to
that standard. He loved his neighbour as himself.
All the world was to be like him shouting his joy, and
the thrill of his triumph in the march of the great machine.
One day the whole world will be lighted by electric light,
have hot and cold water laid down in all the houses,
have bath tubs and central heat in universal use and ride
everywhere in automobiles.

He beamed upon us as that glorious vision passed
before his eyes, and we beamed back at him for his
enthusiasm was infectious. But as I looked around
the faces in the room I saw that there were some that
doubted, and I was glad because I doubted too. There
was another side to this picture. This greatness of

The Great Commandment

America had cost and was costing something. A man's happiness consisteth not in the multitude of things that he possesseth. What profit was it to a man or a nation to gain the whole world and lose his own soul? And the only thing that was peculiarly American about the speech was its openness and honesty. The creed was the common creed of industrialism, industrialism in its finest form inspired by public spirit. No mean petty selfishness here.

The American business man, he said with triumph, was not in business for the love of money. He was in it for the love of the game, for the power and satisfaction that the very business brought. This man loved his neighbour as he loved himself. He loved me as he loved himself. He wanted to give himself to me. Awful thought! because I did not want him. I did not want him a bit. Nay, I hate the whole idea in my heart with a bitter hatred, and yet he was a good man. He loved his neighbour as himself, and here he was sincerely trying to do good and make all the world as rich as possible. Why was I not attracted? He had a different god. That was it. It was not about the second commandment that we differed. It was about the first. He loved himself in a different way and loved his neighbour in a different way because he worshipped a different god. He was really deeply religious. He loved his god with all his heart, with all his soul (that was the awful part of it) and with all his mind, and there was quite a lot of that. He had a prodigious memory for figures and a first rate intellect, and he loved his neighbour as himself. And when I looked at his large, powerful, sallow face with huge horn spectacles I could not really believe that this man was sound in body and soul. His religion was false and that made his ethics all wrong too. His love for his neighbour was all to be measured in dollars because the dollar was his god, and that's just it.

Your love for your neighbour can only be measured in terms of your god. Everyone has a god even the, poor old drunkard has his creed. " I believe in alcohol almighty, maker of heaven and joy on the earth, in good red wine, his only son, who gives men love and laughter and the beauty of bright eyes, and in the potent spirit, giver of life, who lifts the fainting to their feet and makes the coward's heart feel brave." He loves his neighbour as himself. There is a world-wide fellowship of wine. He does his duty to his god and his neighbour when he says, " Come and 'av a drink."

Everyone has a god. Your god is what you live for, and a man must live for something, and it is what you live for that makes you what you are, and that determines the value of the love you bear your fellowmen.

The second commandment has no meaning and no value apart from the first. It is entirely dependent upon it. The truth of the matter is that the man in the street is a fool who can only be answered according to his folly. The sort of claptrap which he uses to excuse himself from the task of thinking is not so much untrue as nonsensical. As we would expect Jesus Christ is manifestly right. By far the most important thing in your life is your god, and your relation to him.

It is possible for a man to be a theoretical atheist and live because his god may be his truth, and he will give his negative god away and strive to make all his neighbours atheists because he loves them as he loves himself. A militant atheist is a contradiction in terms. You cannot fight unless you have something to fight for, and if you have something to fight for, that is if you are militant, you are not an atheist. Even militant agnosticism is difficult. An agnostic either worships his own ignorance, which is often a cloak for his own superior mind, or else he worships truth, and goes out to defend it against lies. A thoroughgoing agnostic cannot even know that he cannot know. He cannot even be sure that he is alive. Real atheism and agnosticism do not need a philosopher to help them. They need a physician. They suffer from mental diseases. It is quite certain that man must have a god to love or gods. The only question is what those gods shall be.

Why Sin ?

WHY did I do it ? How could I have done it ? These can be the bitterest and most tragic questions men and women ask themselves. Something done that cannot be undone, something final and irrevocable, and a man looks at it, and cannot recognise it as his own act, cannot see himself in it, and yet knows that it is his, and must be his for ever.

> So Judas must have looked on Christ,
> As from the Judgment hall He went
> In bonds, the blood still wet upon
> His back. Why did I do it ? How
> Could I have done it ? I loved Him,
> Yet I sold Him. How can that be ?
> Which am I—traitor—lover—friend
> Or fiend incarnate ? Am I mad ?
> Aye mad—stark mad—my reason rocks.
> These coins are bloody—Jesus help !
> I did not mean to do it. Bloody—
> Wet and bloody—and they burn—hot.
> Hot as hell. I cannot bear it.
> I am not I. I am some damned
> And dreadful thing spewed out of hell.
> I am—and I must kill it—now.
> I cannot live—it must go back
> To hell—I must—and never see
> Him—never—Jesus Mercy ! Death—
> I must find death.

Why Sin?

Remorse and repentance are human facts, peculiarly human facts. Of no other creature could that scene be true, but only of a man. It might be true of you or me. Quite ordinary people can feel like that, and do. I have seen them, sat with them, tried to comfort them. I have heard them muttering over and over again. How could I have done it? How could I have done it?

Well—how could they? Why did they? It is no good saying to them "Never mind. It is done now, and cannot be helped. You made a mistake, and everybody makes mistakes." It is no good talking like that because it is not true, and they know it is not true. This was not a mistake, it was a sin, and they know it. A sin is more than a mistake, and deep down within him every man who has a deep-down knows that it is more than a mistake. It is one thing to kick oneself as a fool, and another to curse oneself as a sinner. In both cases there is a cleavage in the self, but a mistake is a cleavage of the surface, a sin is a cleavage that cuts down to the very depths. The shallow man or woman who is all surface and no depths can treat sins as mere mistakes. The fool can say in his heart that there is no God, but he must be an awful fool. There are many such fools in the world, and for them sin has no meaning. They cannot be conscious of a cleavage in their deepest self because they have no real self to cleave. They have no character, and it takes a character to sin, and know himself a sinner. But character must be formed. We are not born with it ready-made. We are born with the raw material out of which it can be made. We inherit a howling mob of powerful but disorganised desires and disgusts, natural attractions and repulsions, and the purpose of our lives is to organise this mob into a disciplined and working union.

Sin comes when some desire with a very loud voice breaks away from the union or refuses to come in, and tricks us into doing something of which the union, the partly organised self, thoroughly disapproves. The sense of sin is strong if inward union is strong, and weak if it is weak. Thousands of people have no sense of sin because they are still just howling mobs inside. Their desires clamour and bawl against one another, and the one with the loudest voice gets his way for a moment even though it is a silly fool of a desire that ought to shut his mouth and keep still. We all know such people. They are the despair of decent men. Their promises are like pie-crusts, and they never know their own minds from day to day. They cannot see any sense in this talk about sin, it is to them perfectly meaningless. Sin is disloyalty to the inward union of desires, and they have not got a union to be disloyal to. They may be clever, even brilliant people, but that only makes it worse. Their wits are the willing servants of their desires. They cannot lead them to the truth, they only lead to " lawyer's truth," making out a good case for what, at the moment, they want to be true.

Out of such people it is impossible to form a society in the true sense of that word, a social unity. You cannot form a society except out of social people, and social people must each one of them have some sort of union within, or they can never form any outward unity. They must have some common pupose and life aim round which, as individuals, they seek to organise, and in which, as a society, they seek to centre, their conflicting desires. That is they must have some common conviction as to the meaning and purpose of life. Custom and convention may hold them together for a while, they live then on the relics of dead or dying convictions. But that cannot last long. Convention

which has no vital conviction behind it is like dead
wood, it snaps when it is strained, and not even law is
strong enough to hold it together if conviction really
goes. That is why a sense of sin is in the end a social
necessity. The disappearance of it means the break of
the inner union of desires, it means a decay in the conviction of a common purpose in life, and that decay
finally destroys even convention, and the result of that
is anarchy and chaos.

That is the bad side of the rebellion against convention, which we see around us everywhere to-day. It
proceeds, at any rate in part, from the death amongst us
of any common conviction as to the meaning and
purpose of life, and that, if it continues, can only result
in social ruin. The idea of liberty which is dominant
in our modern world is subject to most mischievous
perversions. Even religious teachers have unwittingly
helped to pervert it by teaching that the essence of
liberty is the power to choose between good and evil,
but the power to choose evil is merely the power to die,
if it can be called a power. It is nothing but the possibility of death and decay. A man cannot be really free
unless he surrenders himself utterly and without reserve
to the service of the highest. The real tyrants which
cramp and cabin man are his own undisciplined and
unorganised desires. He cannot be free except through
the inner union of his passions, without that the only
freedom he possesses is freedom to hang himself. However much rope you give him that is what he must use
it for in the end, unless he has some great aim and purpose
which gives meaning and unity to his life. If he has
that aim and purpose, and his desires are organised and
disciplined about it, then when he acts against that aim
and purpose, when he forgets it, and follows some
wayward and rebellious passion, there comes to him

the sense of sin. He knows that there is something awful, something deadly, about the word or deed. It is not merely a piece of folly, a mistake, a sin against himself or his neighbour, it is a denial of the whole meaning of the world. It is a sin against his God.

That is the essence of sin, it is always an offence against a man's God, whatever God it be. A man's God—his real God—is that which gives meaning and purpose to his life. The God may be a Goddess, a girl, many a man has known the sense of sin first because he was disloyal to the woman he loved, and in whom his real self was centred. She made all the difference between a mistake and a sin. She made possible for him the sense of sin, repentance, and remorse, because she was the real centre of his soul. If the oft-quoted saying of Sir Oliver Lodge is true, and the modern man is not worrying about his sins, it is, I fear me, because he has no high God to sin against. It is because life has lost its centre, and largely lost its sense. It tends to be " Just one damned thing after another," to use a very expressive if vulgar phrase, and, in a world like that, it is nonsense talking about sin, because it is nonsense talking about any great reality. Goodness, Beauty, Truth, Honour, Virtue, all alike are meaningless, and, of course, there is no sin. A thing may be foolish, inexpedient, inconsiderate, it may be socially harmful or bad policy, it may be a crime or a blunder, but it cannot be a sin. The only thing to do is to forget, to forgive oneself and go on. But the man who has a God knows that he cannot forgive himself, he must be forgiven. He cannot forget, he must remember and atone. He has sinned against something or someone other than and greater than himself, he has cut himself off from the source of his power and peace, and he must

Why Sin ?

get back again. That man has a soul, and knows that
he is in danger of destroying it, and he is the only kind
of man out of which a society can be built, he can
unite with others because he can become united within
himself.

Salvation from Sin

THE attempt to find or found an infallible institution has meant the death of real religion. It has lead to a mechanical idea of the Sacrament of Absolution which has largely destroyed its efficacy. The Church, secure in its ecclesiastical orthodoxy, or anxiously and ingeniously defending it, has neglected or been distracted from its proper business of destroying evil, and effectively absolving or freeing people from the power of sin. And sinners in their desperation have turned to gross superstition or to the New Psychologists for help and healing which they did not get in their Church.

Thousands of men and women, many of them young men and women, are seeking from Freud and Jung what they ought to find in Christ. This may be partly their fault. There is more than a smack of the Athenian about the modern youth, both of the male and female variety ; they dearly love something new. Moreover the New Psychology is " scientific " and the authority of " Science " is a power to conjure with in these days. Formerly people took the priest on trust and followed blindly where he lead, nowadays the scientist has taken his place, and it is assumed that what is claimed to be scientific must be true. The authority of the doctor is more absolute than that of the priest, and the New Psychologist comes in under his wing, so to speak. It is no use complaining about this charge. The Scientist has largely won his authority because he produced results, and we have largely lost ours because we did not. But neither of us is really doing the job. The conclusions of the New Psychology are very tentative, and its methods of healing largely experimental ; and the results of the craze for Psychoanalysis are in many cases disastrous. The cure seems worse than the disease. It is clear that the practice of what is called psycho-therapeutics by enthusiastic amateurs is full of really appalling dangers, and that even in the hands of experts it requires caution and careful handling. Nevertheless it is there, and has come to stay. If some of the conclusions are tentative, there appears to be a solid residuum of ascertained truth, and if much of the method is experimental it does in many cases produce wonderful results.

And these results as far as they go are exactly the results which religion ought to produce. Men and women are set free from the bondage of bad habits, from fears and depressions which have driven them into much that we call, and rightly call, sin. Bitterness, jealousy, envy, hatred, malice, and all uncharitableness, as well as positive vice, may all spring from and be due to some suppression or complex, and may disappear when the complex is dissolved. If absolution means anything it includes in its meaning freedom from the power of these sins. Doubtless Absolution first of all means restoration of the soul to communion with God, but if that restoration is effective it ought to carry with it liberation, from the power of evil. If men and women find that they can obtain that liberation from the Psychoanalyst, which they fail to obtain from the Church, then they will turn more and more to him for help in their trouble.

Well, you say, so long as they obtain it, what does it matter where. The Psychoanalyst is God's minister as the doctor is, and in his sphere is doing priestly work.

It is only another proof that you cannot confine God's mercy within the channels which you choose to suppose are the orthodox ones. The power which the Analyst wields is every bit as much God's power, as the power of the priest. Far be it from me to call good evil or to deny that so far as the Analyst heals men of sin and sickness he is doing God's work, and doing it by God's power; but there are other considerations. Redemption, as we have seen, means not only that men " do not perish " but that they have " everlasting life," not only that they are saved from degeneracy but are given a higher order of life, they are not merely rescued but completed. Now supposing we admit that the Analyst does heal men and women of mental sickness which is the cause of much that we call sin, and that his work is so far good, has he the power of completing that work, and lifting life on to a higher level altogether ?

Healing on the lower level may often be a dangerous thing for the man or woman looked at as an immortal soul. Without for one moment casting any aspersion on the good work of the medical profession, it is doubtful whether they do not cause as well as cure disease, whether the constant suggestion of sickness with which we are to-day surrounded, and our readiness to have recourse to medicine for its cure, does not lead us at times to postpone or refuse that radical alteration in our whole way of living and thinking which would really lead us to health. The divorce of the functions of the doctor and the priest is in many ways dangerous to both. These considerations apply very forcibly to the Analyst and the nerve specialist as they do to the medical practitioner. If one studies and understands the power of repeated suggestion upon the human mind, the wholesale publication of comparatively cheap books on Psychoanalysis and their large circulation is alarming. The continual discussion among young people of the subject has led in my experience to very unpleasant results, and has proved to be the very reverse of elevating.

From the Christian point of view, what the Analyst is really doing is to dissect the carnal mind, and by observing its behaviour over a wide field and tabulating his results to discover, or attempt to discover, the laws by which it works, and so cure its diseases. The process, it is admitted by all, leads one into strange places. We go down with Freud into the very depths, and it is difficult to prevent a feeling of nausea and sickness as one proceeds. Of course the obvious reply to that is that the healer must be prepared to deal with sickening things, the surgeon must open the abscess and let out the filth it contains. An operation to a layman is a sickly business. If there is all this hidden ugliness in the depths of the human mind it is better to face the facts, and get down to it. Because a thing is unpleasant it is not therefore untrue. We must not be turned away from the pursuit of important truths because they lead us into evil smelling places. It is the continual emphasis on the sex impulse that makes much of Freud's work so unpleasant to read, but as he himself observes, Society can conceive of no more powerful menace to its culture than would arise from the liberation of the sexual impulses and a return of them to their original goal. Therefore society dislikes this sensitive place in its development being touched upon ; that the power of the sexual instinct should be recognised, and the significance of the individual's sexual life revealed, is very far from its interests ; with a view to discipline it has rather taken the course of diverting attention from the whole field. For this reason the revelations of psycho-analysts are not tolerated by it, and it would greatly prefer to brand them, as æsthetically offensive, morally reprehensible or dangerous. . . . It is characteristic of human nature to be inclined to regard anything which is disagreeable as untrue, and then, without much difficulty, to find arguments against it. But such objections are not valid arguments against conclusions which claim to represent objective results of scientific investigation.

Now all that is absolutely true, and it is intensely hard to rid one's mind of prejudice. One must admit the right of the pure Scientist to investigate anything, and if this investigation is necessary for the cure of the many moral and nervous disorders which afflict us we must be grateful to the men who undertake it. But if the claims of Christianity are true it ought not to be necessary. We ought to be able to cure these disorders in the name and by the power of Christ. We ought to be able to deliver man from bondage to the carnal mind which we hold to be at enmity with God. And I do believe that a real religious revival would make the whole of this investigation unnecessary from the healing point of view. That the sex impulse does play an absolutely leading part in the carnal mind is evident to any casual observer. Its power to dominate and obsess men and women is undoubted and indisputable. But that it is necessary to analyse and probe into the working of the carnal mind in order to free men from it, or that it is worth analysing for its own sake, is very doubtful. That this analysis is necessary is an assumption. Christianity declares that the carnal mind can be destroyed by the pouring in of the New Life. From a psychological point of view it definitely joins itself to the " Suggestionists " as opposed to the " Analysts "—it declares that what the Analyst takes to be facts are not facts at all but distortions, and that they can be destroyed without analysing and observing them by the Inspiration of the Holy Spirit.

Salvation from Sin

The Christian method of cure is as to its method—Suggestion. The New Nancy school, of which M. Coué is Moses and Badouin Aaron, has rediscovered and re-emphasised the basic truth of the Faith, that ultimately it is what you worship rather than what you will that makes you what you are. It is what dominates your imagination, fills your thoughts, what haunts you, so to speak, that determines your character and action. This is to repeat the experience of S. Paul, " The good that I will to do, I do not. The evil that I will not to do, I do. O wretched man that I am, who will deliver me from the body of this death. Thanks be to God, who giveth us the victory through Jesus Christ our Lord." This is the psychological truth underlying the doctrine of Salvation by faith and not by works. The other name of that doctrine might be Salvation by worship and not by will. An effort of pure will means a divided mind—part of us suggests that we can—part of us that we can't, and the suggestion of impotence wins ; but when a man has found his God, he cries : " I can do all things through Christ which strengtheneth me." This is the Christian method of Salvation.

To say of course that Christianity is only suggestion is to confuse the method with the power. Suggestion is a method not in itself a power, it can be used for evil as well as for good, and in fact is at present much more commonly used for evil than for good. We are subject every day to a continual battery of suggestion. If God works by suggestion so do the world, the flesh, and the Devil, and it is a doubtful point as to how far the Analyst when he cures does not work by suggestion too. How far is it the continual suggestion of a cure that in the end has power to heal rather than the analysis ? The problem of the healing of sickness and sin boils down at last to the question of how to overcome evil suggestion by good. The claim of the Christian Church is that within the Christian Brotherhood there is the Eternal Life, the way of worship, which can through faith in and worship of God revealed in Jesus Christ completely counter the power of evil suggestion, destroy its results, and set the sinner on his feet again. Nor, thank God, is this claim without evidence to back it. If the Christian Church is weak in its positively redemptive work, if she fails to save the sick and sinful as she should, yet it remains true that she is the greatest preventative power against the ravages of sin that the world contains. Millions of men and women are preserved and healed of sin and disease of the mind in its early stages by her ordinary worship, the ministration of the Word and sacraments. That is a fact, I think, beyond dispute. What we must realise is that the tremendous power of mass suggestion which we call the world can only be countered and its victims cured, if they are received into a body which is filled with a vivid, vigorous, and conscious community life of the Spirit. Individuals are powerless to cope with a power so subtle and all pervasive as this mass suggestion is. Catholics have supposed that the Analyst with his discoveries supported them in their practice of self-examination, and conclusively proved its necessity. But from an analytic point of view the ordinary self examination is merely playing with the thing. It is at best an examination of the conscious mind and memory, and does not touch the roots of evil in the subsconscious at all.

Catholics and Protestants alike are from the psychological point of view suggestionists. But the strength of the Catholic position lies in the fact that they have never really surrendered the Community life of the Church, although many " Catholic " Churches, so called, are more protestant than the Protestants, and in practice are as individualist as they can be. Men and women like the ritual and the music, and go to get comfort for themselves, or to indulge in the worship of a God who has no connection with their daily lives, and no work for them to do in the world. The weakness of our redemptive work is due to the weakness of our community life, due to the fact that we are not putting first things first, and bringing forth the fruits of the spirit. If we are to save and rescue sinners there must grow up in our Church a spirit of Love and Brotherhood, a Christian social life transcending class and national distinctions, as pungent, as powerful, as impossible to escape as the Spirit of the world. No Apostolic Succession, no ecclesiastical correctness, no rigidity of orthodox doctrine, can by themselves and in themselves give us this; it comes, and can only come from a clearer vision of the Christ, and more complete surrender to His call, and the bearing of His Cross.

God can and does forgive us our trespasses but only as we forgive them that trespass against us—that is only as we become members of a Church really militant here on earth—which is out to bear in its body the sin of the world.

Man shall not Live by Bread Alone

S. Matt. iv, 4

BEFORE Christ blew the trumpet He had planned out His campaign. He practised what He preached and, as He Himself once said, " What king sets out to fight another king without first sitting down to deliberate whether with ten thousand men he can encounter the king who is attacking him with twenty thousand ? " In their desire to do the heart of Jesus honour many of his most faithful followers underrate His head. We do not understand Him unless we constantly remember that He was a thinker, the deepest and the clearest thinker that the world has ever known. He may have been, I believe He was more than a genius, but He certainly was a genius—an intellectual as well as a moral and religious genius.

When He went out to face the world, He had thought out what He was going to do and how He was going to do it. We do not know, and have no means of knowing, exactly what passed through his mind as He did the work of a carpenter and watched the world in Nazareth. Do not imagine, however, that Nazareth was a peaceful secluded village out of the way of the world. It was nothing of the kind. It was a busy place where great roads met, and there was a constant coming and going of caravans and travelling traders in its streets. Eastern merchants jostled Roman soldiers in its crowded market place, for the Roman legions passed and repassed through it on their journeys south and north. In and out amongst them as boy and man went the carpenter of Nazareth, wide-eyed, observant, wondering. As one of his closest friends has said, "He knew man and did not need anyone to tell Him what was in man." He was under no delusions. He knew the blindness and brutality He was up against. He knew that he would have a job to make these Jew folk see the Truth as He saw it. The world through the windows of Nazareth did not look like the Kingdom of God. The flesh and the devil were hot and strong. The prostitute with her painted face put up her wares for sale, and the rough-tongued burly Roman soldiers crowded round to buy. The proud and pious Pharisee, like a ship in full sail, came strutting down the street to prayer, and did not see the large-eyed child that whimpered cries for bread. There was the clerk to the synagogue in his long robes. He owned a neighbour's house, and when the husband died, and the widow could not pay the rent, he turned her out, and read the lesson on the Sabbath day (S. Mark, xii. 40). Such men as he devoured widows' houses and grew fat and were much respected.

The Carpenter looked on and wondered at it all, and often His heart was hot within him. There had been, we know, an attempted revolution in His time. He had heard the wild speeches of the leaders and seen the ragged mob swarm after them with broken swords and pruning hooks. Then came the legions marching like a great machine. There were cries and bloodshed in the streets, and the trembling people saw their leaders flogged and tied to the horses' tails on their way to crucifixion. He had lived through stirring times, and His keen brain and observant eyes missed nothing of what they had to tell. He read the Jewish scriptures, and the history of his people. He knew and loved their poetry and learned by heart their psalms. He wandered off by himself to the hills where He could catch a glimpse of the sea and watch great ships go by. And all the time He was thinking, thinking, thinking.

At last He felt that His time had come and He must act. He went down south to hear His cousin John the Baptist preach on the banks of the river Jordan. The preaching stirred Him deeply, and He sat with the crowd and watched the rugged prophet's face as he poured forth his denunciation of their sins, and his call to true repentance. He took His place with the rest in the queue to be baptized in the blue waters of the Jordan. His cousin knew Him, and was troubled. As He came down the bank into the water, the Baptist whispered, " This is not for You," but Jesus insisted, " Yours is a call from God," He said, " and I answer, like the rest."

It was just after His cousin's baptism that there came one of the great experiences of His life. Always during those years at Nazareth, He had been conscious of the presence of God and the conviction that He was called to some great and special work for God had been growing upon Him. He had His hours of doubt and bewilderment, but the certainty and the urgency of the call increased. It was that which had driven Him from home, and brought Him here to the river side. But now as He sprang, naked and glowing, from the water, He had an inner experience impossible to put into words. We have memories of His own description of it preserved in the records. It was as though a great light shone round about Him, and a voice within Him cried, " You are my Son and the Joy of my heart " (S. Matthew iii, 17). At the same time, He was conscious of a new power. The Spirit of God moved over His soul as it moved over the face of the waters on the birthday of the world. To read the description of this experience literally, and suppose that there was a human voice that spoke out of the sky, or a feathered dove that floated down, is to read poetry as prose, and to rob the record of its manifest reality and power. It was an inner experience which constituted a turning point in the greatest and most epoch-making life that has ever been lived on earth. In that, and not in its apparently miraculous form, lies its importance to the history of man.

The effect of the experience on Jesus was to make Him feel that the time for action had arrived. The certainty that He was called to do a unique work and was endowed with unique powers burned now like a fire within Him. He hurried away from the Jordan to the lonely and desolate region that lies beyond it. In the graphic language of the records " he was led by the Spirit into the wilderness to be tempted by the devil " (St. Matthew iv. 1). Once more you deprive the Gospel account of its reality and power if you take it literally and imagine the temptation in the wilderness as a dialogue between a plain and obvious devil, with horns and hoofs and all the appurtenances thereof, and Christ.

Jesus was alone, as utterly alone as a man can be. Had you passed that way you would have seen nothing but a solitary pale-faced majestic Jew sitting on a rock, or pacing up and down some rugged path lost in thought. But no one is ever really alone. Loneliness is a feeling, not a fact. The blind man may say there is no sun, but the light still blazes round him. The deaf man may say there is no sound, but the chorus of the summer woods swells on and is not stilled. The lonely man may say " I am alone," but God and his fellow men are all about him, his loneliness is in himself. He is lonely because he is not fully alive and awake and cannot

191

realise the truth. But Jesus was fully alive and awake, and therefore He was never alone. God and the world were always with Him. He carried them both together in His Heart and in His Head. We all can carry God and the world in our hearts and heads to a certain extent, and the greater our power of doing that, the more universal our sympathy and thought is, the greater we are as men and women.

It is because Jesus of Nazareth impresses us as having powers of universal thought and feeling which were unique and unparalleled that we say His humanity was divine. There in the wilderness He was nearer to God and more closely united with His fellow men than He was in the streets of Nazareth. He went away from them that He might draw them closer in. But he who carries God and the World in his heart and head must suffer. There must inevitably arise within him a conflict, and the greater his power of thought and feeling, the greater that conflict is. This inner conflict is inevitable because the world is partly ugly and evil, while God is wholly good and beautiful.

The man who knows and loves both God and the world must, therefore, suffer, and endure an inward conflict. It was that inward conflict which was tearing the soul of Jesus as He sat alone. Just because He loved God and the World. He was up against the ugliness and evil in the world. He was quite certain that in reality the world was the Kingdom of God, and that if men could see it as it really is, if they could be awakened out of the sleep of the animal life, and look around them with open eyes and open ears ; then the ugliness and evil would pass away as a hideous dream disappears at the touch of Love's awakening. But how were their eyes to be opened and their ears to be unstopped ?

*   *   *   *   *

Man shall not Live by Bread Alone

With the problem of evil as we put it to ourselves, Jesus never seems to have concerned Himself at all. He never asked Himself " Why is there any evil in the world ? " or " Where does evil come from ? " He has nothing to tell us about the origin of evil. He never tried to explain it even to Himself. He was entirely absorbed in destroying it. He called it " Satan," or " the adversary," and His only concern with it was to tear and root it out of the world.

It is impossible to say whether He believed in a personal devil, or not. He talked about him as a person, but that is a natural form of speech. He once called poor old Peter " Satan." But He certainly did not mean that literally. He gives the reason quite clearly to Peter. He called him Satan because he was thinking mean cowardly thoughts, and trying to hold Jesus back from his fight with evil, and the suffering it entailed (S. Matthew xvi, 23). He wanted to make an earthly King of Jesus and put Him on a throne, and, as we shall see, Jesus had decided for very good and sufficient reasons that that was not the way to destroy evil.

The thing we want to grip firmly in our minds is that this temptation in the wilderness was the conflict that He endured in thinking out His plan of campaign, and deciding how men were to be awakened, and made to see that the world is really the Kingdom of God, and wholly good and beautiful, and that the evil was in themselves and could be destroyed.

How were men to be awakened to the Truth and enabled to live it out in their lives ? That was His problem. How was He to get hold of them and make them see ? The first answer that suggested itself was " Feed them." Would it not be best to begin by destroying poverty and want, and giving the people bread ?

This problem of the people's bread was always on His mind, and in His heart. He had lived among the poor. And there in the dim grey light of the morning when the rocks and boulders round Him, by a natural association of ideas grew to look like loaves of bread, He was surrounded, I believe, by an innumerable phantom host of the world's hungry people. He saw them stretching out into the distance like an endless sea. Mothers clasping puny children to their dry and shrivelled breasts ; fathers tearing open their ragged shirts to show the bones beneath their skin, and holding out lean and skinny arms in supplication ; while all around Him, like the moan of the sea, there went up the cry of a world of want, " Bread ! Bread ! For God's sake give us Bread. If thou be the son of God, command these stones that they may become bread." And He, seeing the multitude, had compassion upon them, for divers of them came from afar, so very far, through so many bitter disappointments, with broken boot soles flapping round their feet, along miles and miles of dirty pavement, miles and miles of filthy streets. " Bread ! Bread ! For God's sake give us bread ! " It was the supreme problem of His life, and how was He to solve it ?

He felt within Him the pulse of extraordinary powers. He knew that in some strangely unique and wonderful way He was the Man, the chosen Man.

Imp.

If it ought to be done, He had no doubt it could be done. If it was God's Will then there must be God's Way. Surely this was the most pressing and crying problem. Here was the greatest need, to feed the people. Was it any use giving them God unless He gave them bread ? How could they worship unless they were fed ? Was it not mockery to tell them of a Father's love unless He satisfied their human need ? And yet—He

194

knew man and needed not that anyone should tell him what was in Man.

Intellectual power consists in the capacity to learn by experience, and His intellect was as clear as light itself. He had tried it—this giving men bread. It did not work. What did they do? Snatched it, gobbled it up, lay down in the sun to sleep, and presently came crying for more. Memories of beggars at Nazareth came crowding in upon Him. He saw a beggar eating outside the carpenter's shop, ravenously tearing the loaf with his hands, looking over his shoulder now and then with that furtive look of fear that an animal has when it eats. Jesus was an utter realist. He never allowed His passion, not even His passion of pity to cloud His intellect. He saw right to the heart of the problem of bread, and arrived at clear and definite principles upon which the solution of it must depend.

The first of these principles was the principle of Work. Bread is a curse when it is not earned. Unearned bread, in the end, corrupts both body and soul. It does not wake men from the sleep, or rescue them from the sensual slough of the animal life. It pushes them deeper into it.

Man cannot live on unearned bread. He must work. He must work with and for God and his fellow men, and by working with and for them, learn to love them. It is by work that man must learn to live by every word that proceeds from the mouth of God. That is to say by the eternal principles of justice, honesty, mercy, and mutual love. He must consciously co-operate with God and with his fellow men in the building of the Kingdom, and in the great school of voluntary co-operative service, must learn to value the kingdom more highly than himself. To give men bread without calling upon them to earn it, is to rot them both body and soul.

It was His insight into this great truth which lay behind His horror of riches. It was not that He regarded riches as bad in themselves. He was not a lean, hungry ascetic who despised the good things of the world, and bade men seek for heaven by turning their faces from the earth. That was one of the things His critics and enemies complained about. They called Him a glutton and a drunkard because He ate and drank like other men, and loved a feast with His friends.

What He dreaded about riches was that they took men out of the working fellowship of God and man. They tempted men to believe that they were really independent of God and of their fellow men. They tempted men to live private lives on private means, and that life is damnation because it is a lie. The man who believes that he can really live a private life on his own private property is damned because he is cut off from the family of God which lives by the work of the world. You see this point brought out with perfect clarity when a man who was staying in the crowd, listening to His teaching, cried out, " Master, speak to my brother that he divide the inheritance with me " (S. Luke xii, 13). He saw right through that cry. Here was a man who cared more for the inheritance than he did for the brotherhood. He wanted to use Jesus, nay, he would have used God himself, as a means of getting that bit of property. Both the brothers were probably like that, and there was the root of their trouble. They had lost their brotherhood in their desire for inheritance. You can never satisfy men like that. You cannot give any decision which they will both accept as just, because they really do not want justice, they want the lot.

Jesus went to the root of the trouble when He said, " Take heed and beware of covetousness, for a man's life consisteth not in the multitude of things he

possesseth." Get back to the brotherhood again and
you will soon find a way to divide the inheritance.
Then He told them the story of the rich fool.

He had a run of luck and raked in plenty, and said
to himself, " Now I have any amount of private means
and I can live a private life. I need never do another
hand's turn for anyone as long as I live. I will have a
good time." Then God whispered in his ear, " Thou
fool. This night shall thy soul be required of thee."

I do not believe that that was a summons to death.
I think it was the realisation of the truth that sooner or
later comes to all who live on unearned bread, and cut
themselves off from the working fellowship of the
world ; the truth that easy money is muck that has no
value and no meaning.

It was because the rich man is inevitably tempted to
cut himself off from the fellowship of service, that Jesus
saw that his money was a danger to his manhood. The
same danger, as Jesus clearly saw, exists for the beggars ;
the scrounger who, being able-bodied, is content with
given bread. If Lazarus could work and would not, he
must go to Hell like Dives, because no man can live by
bread alone, not even though he be content with crusts
from a rich man's table.

The clarity of Jesus' vision was unclouded, and He
saw that the rich man who lives without effort in a
world of work was a miserable, poverty-stricken soul,
exactly like the lousy, shiftless, drunken beggar who,
with loose mouth and wandering eye, preys on the pity
of decent men. There was not in His eyes anything to
choose between them. They both were naked outcasts
from God's world of working men.

It is this first principle of work which if honestly
applied would begin the Christian revolution.

* * * * *

The second great principle of Jesus which is con‑
tained in this saying, "Man shall not live by bread
alone, but by every word that proceedeth out of the
mouth of God," is the principle of responsibility, the
responsibility of men to God.

Every power that a man possesses is a trust to him
from God for the use of which he is responsible.
Responsibility was the needle's eye through which the
rich and heavily burdened camel might hope to pass by
the grace of God.

If, in his riches, the rich man recognised an awful
and dangerous responsibility; if he did not allow his
riches to cut him off from the working fellowship of
God and man, but set himself with all his heart and mind
to use them according to God's will and for the glory
of His Kingdom, he might save his soul alive, and hear
God's great "Well done!"

This principle of responsibility is stated clearly by
Jesus in the parable of the talents (S. Matt. xxv. 14).   It
is from this story that the word talent has come to be
used in its present sense of inherited capacity or natural
endowment.   Jesus being a realist recognised the fact
that men are born unequal.   We are by nature differently
and very unequally endowed.   There are, in every
generation, born men of one, two, three, and four
talents.   We are born unequal, and cannot by any system
of education or reform be made equal.

The only way to reduce men all to one level is to
reduce them to a dead level.   We shall never be equal
until we are dead.   We cannot make the man of one
talent equal to the man of four, though we might, by
tryanny and persecution, make the man of four talents
almost equal to the man of one.   We can level men
down, but we can never level them up.

These   natural   and   inevitable   inequalities   are   the cause of much misery and sin, because we use, or fail to use our talents with a sense of responsibility to God.

The man of many talents says, " These are mine to use for myself, and I have a right to use them as I will." The man of one talent says, " What is the good of bothering? Life is unjust and unfair. He has four and I have only one." Tyranny, envy and hatred are the inevitable result. There arises what we in modern times call class war. Our misuse of our national inequalities becomes stereotyped and fixed into our customs, laws and institutions, and social strife and discontent threatens to tear the working fellowship into pieces. We pass laws to restrain the man of four talents, and to protect the man of one.

But the strong man uses his talents to override or get round the laws, and we go round in a circle, and always will, unless we recognise the principle of responsibility. We only break the vicious circle as we get more and more men who look upon every power they possess as a trust from God to be used according to His Will, and for the glory of His Kingdom.

When the principle of responsibility is recognised, then the talented man, the naturally rich man, becomes a public servant. The greatest becomes the servant of all. Instead of allowing his riches to cut him off from the working fellowship of God and Man, the rich man sees that it brings him closer to it. He has much, and therefore owes much to God and man, and he spends his life discharging the debt.

This is the basis of the Christian social order. As Jesus put it to His disciples when they were quarrelling about who should be greatest. " The Kings of the heathen lord it over the people, and call themselves their benefactors. That must not be the way with you. He who is greatest amongst you must count himself as least, and your chief must be the servant of all " (S. Luke xxii, 25).

The third great principle contained in the saying, " Man shall not live by bread alone," is the principle of Purpose. The only way to secure for all a higher standard of life is to set before all a higher purpose for living.

So long as men continue to live the animal life, eating, drinking, lusting, breeding and looking for nothing more, they must live under the law which governs animal life, the law of mutual conflict and death. There is no poverty amongst animals because death, with majestic mercy, lays its great hand unerringly upon the weak and weary and sinks them back on sleep.

Without the Father's knowledge truly no sparrow falls to the ground, and yet the sparrows fall. God does feed the birds of the air, and clothe the lilies of the field, that survive in their natural struggle for existence, but He cannot much more clothe men, unless they seek first the Kingdom of God.

So long as our life purpose remains on the level of the beasts, the law of the beasts must be our law ; the world must be a jungle and hunger be its lord.

Therefore let your first thought be not what ye shall eat, or what ye shall drink, or wherewithal shall ye be clothed, for this is the low life purpose of animals and animal-minded man ; but seek ye first the Kingdom of God, the reign on earth of justice, mercy, honesty and mutual love, and all these things shall be added unto you.

N.B. This principle of purpose is one that we are slow to grasp, and our common-sense view of life, the view, that is, which we accept without examination and act upon without question, is that everyone looks after himself, and minds his own business. It will by force of competition work out for the good of all in the end. Jesus says that it cannot, and will not do anything of the kind. On the contrary, so long as men are content with this low life purpose, and live like the beasts, by bread alone, so long will there be poverty, misery and war upon the earth.

The fallacy which underlies the Gospel of enlightened self-interest as the Saviour of Mankind, is the over optimistic belief that the light is as natural to man and as easily come by as the self-interest. But man's natural self-interest is blind, as blind and blinder than the other passions.

Men do by nature mind their own business, but they do not by nature know what their own business is. They busy themselves often in work which means their own undoing. They spend themselves for that which is not bread, and labour for that which satisfieth not.

The amount of human energy which runs to waste in mutual strife, and in the production of poisonous trash is appalling. If this waste energy were caught up, concentrated upon, and consecrated to a high life purpose, it would be more than sufficient to feed the hungry, clothe the naked, and give the thirsty drink, there would be enough to build the New Jerusalem and pave its streets with gold.

Slowly, very slowly, we are beginning to realise that Jesus was right. We begin to see that so long as with blind eyes and a low life purpose, man strives with man, class with class, and nation with nation, most of the colossal energy that the human race controls runs to waste ; producing only blood and tears, and a dim vision of what could be done if that energy were directed to a noble end, begins to dawn upon us.

The first principles of the Kingdom of God are the only foundations upon which it is possible to build a truly civilised society. They are not impossible ideals, but the only practical rules by which to live.

Man cannot live by given bread. Man needs God's school of honest work, that he may use in that his powers, recognising them as a trust from God given to him for the high and holy purpose of building the Kingdom here on earth. We cannot live our lives on prose, we need the poet's flame of Truth, and a vision of God's purpose.

> "Bring me my bow of burnished gold,
>   Bring me my arrows of desire,
>   Bring me my spear—O clouds unfold—
>   Bring me my chariot of fire.
>   I will not cease from mental strife,
>   Nor shall the sword sleep in my hand,
>   Till we have built Jerusalem.
>   In England's green and pleasant land."

Jesus came to found a Kingdom. He came to found a Kingdom here upon this earth, where fields are green and skies are blue and blood runs red like wine. He was a practical Man and He set about His task in a practical way. Before He went out on the Great adventure He sat down to plan His course of action out. What was He to do? That was the question. In order to found the Kingdom He had to win men to Himself. How was He to win them?

We have seen that the first way which suggested itself to His mind was to feed them. It was the way of bribery. He rejected it and we have seen why. Bribery and corruption go together and He knew it. To give men what they ought to earn is to sap the fibre from their souls. Man shall not live by bread alone, but by every word that proceedeth out of the mouth of God. Bribery would not do. How then was He to win men?

Man shall not Live by Bread Alone

There is another way in which men have, all through the ages, been moved to follow leaders and to found Kingdoms on the earth. It is the way of superstition. Superstitious fear, the dread of the unknown, has been one of the great forces moulding the destiny of man. It is a curse from which, in its cruder forms at any rate, we are now very largely free; but for more years than we have any record of, it played an enormous part in the lives of men. It was this method that Jesus was tempted to employ. There was a legend amongst the Jews that when the Saviour came, He would come floating down from the clouds of heaven to take command of all the earth. Jesus knew Himself to be possessed of extraordinary powers. He had no doubt that He could find a way to do whatever was God's Will. If a miracle was needed to start the Kingdom going, then a miracle could be worked. Suppose He took it that way.

He had a vision of the Temple at Jerusalem glittering like some snow mountain in the sun, and Himself standing on the topmost pinnacle above the thronged and crowded courts. He sees Himself outlined against the sky. Then suddenly He throws Himself over. The ancient promise is fulfilled. God's angels catch and bear Him up and He floats down in majesty before the astounded and awe-stricken multitude. Would they not follow Him then? But He knows man and needs not that anyone should tell Him what is in man.

Magic was not unknown in the East then. It is not unknown in the East to-day. The fakir or miracle monger was a common figure in the crowded streets at feasts and market days. He remembers the look in the faces of a Galilean crowd when some son of the Pharisees had cast out a devil or performed some " miracle " of healing. The momentary hush followed by an outbreak of jabbering and gesticulation as they jostled and pushed one another round the miracle man, yelling for more. They would follow him in crowds, but they would only follow him for what they could see and what they could get. If He performed this great miracle and came down from the Temple's dizzy heights, they would doubtless follow Him in multitudes, but they would follow Him only for the same low reasons. They would crowd round to see the show and get what they could get. It would not make them any better as men and women. It would not change their hearts and minds or make them the kind of people of whom His Kingdom could be built. It would set men looking to God to do things *for* them, instead of looking to Him to do things *in* them and *through* them. It would debase or degrade rather than inspire and uplift them. It would teach them to expect God to work continual miracles for them and get them out of all their difficulties without any effort on their part. They would always be attempting or trying to make God put everything right for them instead of working together to put things right for themselves, "Thou shalt not tempt the Lord, Thy God." That is the curse of false religion, the evil of superstition.

True religion brings out all the good there is in man and sets it to work making the world a better and a lovelier place, building the Kingdom of God. False religion teaches men to leave everything to God and expects Him to build the Kingdom without our aid and over our heads. There is a lot of false religion in the world still. Men still tempt God. They come to Him for what they can get. They pray to Him for what they want, and if they do not get it, then they give up praying altogether, and say it is no good.

Now Jesus was very emphatic in His teaching about

204

prayer. He told us we were to pray and to keep on praying. He evidently never thought that men could live rightly unless they prayed. He told a very human story with a touch of fun in it about prayer. There was a man who had locked up for the night and gone to bed with his wife and children when a friend came knocking at the door and wanting to borrow a loaf of bread. The man very naturally told him to get out of that and not come bothering him at that time of night, but the friend kept on knocking at the door and saying how badly he wanted this loaf. It was not for himself, he said, but for someone who had turned up to visit him. At last the man got so sick of the knocking that he got up and handed out the loaf. It is a homely, human story, and the point of it is that the builders of the Kingdom must persistently pray to God.

But if you take His pattern prayer, and read His teaching in the light of it, you begin to see that the purpose of prayer with Jesus was not to get God to do things for you, but to enable God to do things in you and through you. The purpose of prayer with Jesus was to make you a better, finer man or woman through whom God could work His Will and build His Kingdom on earth. Our Father who art in Heaven, Hallowed be Thy Name. Thy Kingdom come on earth as it is in Heaven. Thy Will be done on earth as it is in Heaven. In order that we may do Thy Will give us—*us*, mind you, not *me*—our daily Bread. Forgive us our sins against Thee as we forgive them that sin against us. Lead us not into Temptation—but if in the course of duty, temptation comes, deliver us from evil. We turn to Thee for help and inspiration because There is the Kingdom, from Thee alone can come the power enabling us to build it, and in Thee is all its glory that is to be revealed through us in this world, and the worlds beyond for all eternity.

When you pray like Jesus it is clear that you are not asking God to do things for you, you are asking God to give you the desire and the power to do things for Him. That is a different story, isn't it? Jesus taught that there was no good thing which God does not desire to give us. The difficulty lies in preparing ourselves to receive, to appreciate, and to use rightly the gifts that He is striving to impart. The tragedy arises from the fact that God cannot give us more than we prepare ourselves to receive. There are in each and all of us unknown and immense capacities for good. We are, indeed, if we would only realise it, the sons of God. All the treasures of an infinite universe of goodness, truth and beauty are ours if we will set ourselves with single minds to seek the highest. But we must ask and keep on asking, we must seek and keep on seeking ; we must knock and keep on knocking. Only to those who persevere can the glory of the Kingdom be revealed. The difficulty according to Jesus does not lie in persuading God to give, but in preparing ourselves to receive. The Kingdom of God, the fairer, finer, cleaner world is ours as we ourselves develop our longing and desire for it.

This was the very core of Jesus' teaching. God is good and desires our good. He could not and would not ever do us any harm. God loves us whether we love Him or not. He loves His enemies. That is why we must love our enemies. Jesus said, " The old teachers used to tell you to love your friends and hate your enemeis, but I tell you to love your enemies, bless the man that curses you, do a good turn to the chap that hates you, put up a prayer for those that have a spite against you, and seek to hurt you. That is the only way you can be like God, your Father. He does not ask whether a chap is a saint or a scoundrel before He sends him sunshine. He serves them all alike because He loves them all alike.

Anybody can like those that like him. That is easy. It is liking the other fellow when he does not like you that is the rub. Trying to turn your enemies into friends, that is the job. That is what we must do because it is God's job ; it is what God is always doing. That is what shocked and surprised people about the teaching of Jesus. He was so broad-minded, friendly, and human, and He made God so broad-minded, friendly and human. People could not believe it then. They cannot altogether believe it now. A God of power they could understand. A God who could work miracles and prove His Power, punishing His enemies, and rewarding His friends that they might worship and follow because they would be afraid of Him. They would follow Him for what they could get, and in order to insure themselves against His anger. A God like that is awkward to deal with when He starts throwing His weight about, and they would feel that it was prudent to keep on the right side of him. There has always been a lot of that sort of religion knocking about the world ; there is still. God pays His debts without money, people think. Look out or He'll get you. If He does not get you here He'll get you hereafter. It is safer to keep in with God. As an old fellow in a play I once saw says to his son, " Mark my words, my lad, God is a fair stickler for His position. 'E will 'ave proper respec'. And if tha says boo to 'Im 'E'll say a fat sight more than boo to thee, an 'e never forgets nowt, 'E don't, never forgets nowt. Tread on 'Is toes, my lad, and 'E'll tread on thine until tha squeals 'ell out of 'eaven, and then there's a great gulf fixed, as the old

Book says. If 'E gets thee there 'E's got thee fair and there'll be no shiftin' quarters."

That is something like the way in which many people have always thought about God. But it is not Jesus' way. He wanted to lead men not to the fear but to the love of God. It would not have served His purpose to terrify or overcome people by display of miraculous power. That would not have changed their hearts or made them love one another. He wanted to make men hate evil, not fear the punishment of evil. He wanted to make them love Good ; not the reward of being good.

There was only one way for Him. He had to show men what real goodness is like, and earn their love. That was the way He chose. He acted as He believed God would, if He were a man.

That is what led Him to reject the third and last way of winning men which presented itself to Him, as He sat and pondered over His plan of campaign in the wilderness. The third and last way was the way of the sword.

If He could not bribe men by giving them bread, or awe them by working miracles, could He not force them by wielding the sword ?

It was the way by which up to His time all Kings had chosen to found and consolidate their kingdoms. It was, moreover, the way His own people would expect Him to take. They were expecting a military Messiah, and there could be no doubt that they would follow Him if He set up His standard and called for volunteers.

This way made a very strong appeal to His natural ambition. Jesus was human, and we cannot suppose that He was without ambition. He was a great man, remember. He was a greater and more magnetic personality than Napoleon. He felt the power within

208

Him. Great men do. He longed for a chance to work His Will upon the world. He had a vision of the Kingdoms of the earth and all the glory of them. He could add to that glory. He could make it real. Why should He not take that way? He Himself, by His own power has made us feel that it was impossible for Him to take it, but there was nothing to make it clear that the way of the sword was not God's way. The men of His time would have said unanimously and without hesitation that it was God's way, and that He would have been right to take it.

Jesus was a patriot. He loved His own land and His own people with a deep and passionate love, as all fine men must do. His love for the Holy Land and the Holy City burns its way still through the ages. " O Jerusalem, Jerusalem, that stonest the prophets and killest them that are sent unto thee, how often would I have gathered thy children together as a hen doth gather her brood under her wings, and thou would'st not. O if thou had'st, even thou, in this thy day, the things that belong unto thy peace. But now are they hid from thine eyes."

The passion of that cry has its way with us yet, and it is hard to read it unmoved. He loved His people, and they were oppressed and down-trodden. The insolent, swaggering, all-conquering Romans trampled them under foot. They groaned under a crushing load of unjust taxation, and the children cried for bread. Was it not high time that someone struck a blow for freedom in his country's cause? Would not any strong man's heart burn within him, and his hand instinctively feel to find his sword.

We know that the temptation came to Jesus, and by the way He tells the story we can guess that it was a fierce and fiery temptation.

His heart did burn within him. His hand did feel instinctively to find His sword. He was a warrior by nature, and came of a warrior race. He had soldier's blood in His veins. It did not count for nothing that He was David's son. But He rejected the way of the sword more fiercely than either of the other two. There is a kind of cold fury in the words, " Get thee behind Me, Satan." They have passed into a proverb of repulsion and disgust.

We can measure the power of the appeal which the temptation made to Him by the ferocity with which He rejected it. But why did He decide against the sword ? Was it because He felt Himself unable to wield it, and saw only failure staring Him in the face if He tried ? Was He afraid ? That would contradict the whole of His life. He appears to have feared nothing and no one on earth. Fearlessness is one of His outstanding characteristics.

If He had believed it was God's Will, I do not think He would have hesitated. What would have been the result ? Who can tell ? Here was one greater than Napoleon. Who can tell ?

European history might have read differently. The armies of the Carpenter might have hurled a Roman Cæsar from his throne. Whatever way He chose, we may be sure He would have made history, this solitary Jew in the wilderness, who saw in a moment of time all the Kingdoms of the Earth, and the glory of them.

But He deliberately rejected the way of the sword. He would not even use it as Abraham Lincoln used it, as Benito Mussolini claims to have used it, to save their countries from ruin, and build a goodly state. He was a patriot, but not a sentimental patriot. He was a realist, and went to the root.

These Romans were not the real oppressors of His

people. They were themselves oppressed. They were but slaves who bullied slaves. Cæsar was neither here nor there. If they cast off the Roman yoke they would bind another on their own necks more galling still. They would make a Jewish Cæsar. Make Him one, perhaps. Dress Him up in purple and fine linen, and put Him in a palace to sit upon a throne, chief slave in a world of slaves.

No! Let them pay their pence to Cæsar. He must win their souls to freedom and to God. And the sword was no use for that purpose.

There could be no freedom by the sword, since the sword was the sign of slavery. They that take the sword must perish by the sword, for they are the slaves of fear. He saw that two thousand years ago. We have not seen it yet. There is a dim light dawning, but it is still dark. We cannot see it because we are still afraid. The old savage terror still lurks in the secret places of our souls, and keeps us in bondage. Therefore we wave the Union Jack, sing Rule Britannia, breed vile disease and build Dreadnoughts, because our souls are full of dread.

It was the clear and unclouded perception that force and fear are but two sides of the one thing that made Jesus lay aside the sword as useless. It simply would not and could not serve His purpose. He had to go down to the roots and deliver the human soul from the tyranny of fear. There was only one way of doing that, and that was to teach them the secret of love. Love alone can cast out fear. So by word and deed He set Himself to teach men the way of Love. He bade men fling themselves on life with courage and with confidence, trusting God and trusting one another, consecrating all their energy to the coming of the Kingdom, and He assured them that if they did that all their real wants would be provided for. Much of His teaching still sounds absurdly unpractical and over-optimistic to us because we still are afraid of one another and of life. It sounds absurd to say to men, "Don't worry about what you are to eat and what you are to drink, and what clothes you are to wear. Live like the flowers and the birds." But if you go on to the end it is not so absurd as it sounds.

He does not tell us to sit still and do nothing but try to be like a lily or make a noise like a bird wanting worms. He says that we are to be up and doing. "Seek first the Kingdom of God and His just and honest order of society and you'll get food, drink, and clothes in plenty," He says.

And there is nothing absurd about it. It may not be common sense. But the more common such sense becomes the better it will be for the human race. There is not a doubt that if all the energy of body and mind which is now wasted and frittered away on futile efforts to protect ourselves against our neighbours and secure our selfish interests, to uphold our prestige and credit, and what we are pleased to call our "honour"; if all that energy were redirected to the single and clear-sighted purpose of constructing a just and honest order of society we could satisfy the reasonable wants of every man, woman and child in the world, and have a bit over to play with.

For bed-rock sanity I'll back this economic teaching of Jesus Christ against what millions would call common sense. They would and do turn Jesus' teaching topsy-turvy. They say "Seek ye first what ye shall eat and what ye shall drink and wherewithal ye shall be clothed. In other words make it your first objective to improve your standard of life—and the Kingdom of God will be added unto you." That is what men call common sense, but it is fat-headed, shallow-pated nonsense. It does not and never will work. Materialism is not practical. It inevitably leads to waste and war. The energy that should go into creation is turned to purposes of destruction, and the hungry are not fed. It is the order of the far-off land and not of the Father's Home. Materialism means and must mean that some will waste their substance on riotous living while others sit in tatters and live like herded swine. This common sense of Antichrist issues in South Wales valleys and the Savoy Hotel, in May Day processions of workless workers past the Mayfair Hotel. It is both mean and mad.

He maketh me to lie down in green pastures

" He måketh me to lie down in green pastures,
He leadeth me beside the still waters."

THE very beauty of this picture may only serve to hide
from us the depths of its meaning. We seem to see
the shepherd walking before his flock through fields
decked out with green and gold and all the glory of a
generous God, coming at last to the silent pool with
the reflection of the sky sleeping in its heart, and it
seems as though it were for the glory of the summer and
the sleeping beauty of the pool that the sheep followed
the shepherd. And, indeed, it is for that reason that
many do seek the Good Shepherd. They think of
religion not as a necessity but as a luxury, not as life
but as a kind of addition to life which it is very nice to
have but which we could quite well do without. But
it is not for the green and gold of summer fields that
the sheep seeks to find them, but because they are good
to eat. It is not for the sleeping beauty in the heart of
silent waters that the flock follows on to find them, but
because they are good to drink. It is not luxury that
they ask of the shepherd, it is the bare necessities. And
we cannot make too sure of this, that religion, communion with God, is not luxury but a necessity for the
soul. We must have God.

We are, as we have seen, hungry headed, hungry

hearted, hungry souled, and this intellectual, emotional and spiritual hunger is as tyrannous and terrible if it be not satisfied as the hunger of the body. Many of us are not conscious fully of our hunger of the head and yet it is there. Life lies spread before us like a book— a strange and wonderful book written in characters that we slowly learn to understand—and as year by year we turn its pages over the need to find a meaning in what we read becomes more and more an imperative necessity in our lives. It is literally maddening to be compelled to read a book when here and there there are lines, perhaps lines of perfect beauty, which we can understand and which make us certain that there is a meaning hidden in the whole, and yet, no sooner do our hopes rise high and our eyes begin to shine than we come across a passage which is utterly incomprehensible, and worse than that, looks as though it had been written either by a villain or a fool.

This is like life. It challenges us continually. Challenges our curiosity, our courage, our self-respect. It flings a thousand questions at us and until we begin to die, and we begin to die when we begin to give it up, there is a passionate desire within us to answer the challenge and find the meaning of life. This is the hunger of the head, the hunger for truth and reality, and it must be fed.

Now whatever be the truth that the mind seeks it can only move towards it along one road, and on that road there are three stages. The first is wonder, the second is vision, and the third is venture. There is no other road to the palace of truth but that. Sir Almroth Wright has declared that a pain in the mind is the prelude to all discovery. That is an illuminating phrase. Wonder is a pain in the mind. Sometimes, like many other pains, it seems more like a pleasure at first, a thrill, but if it be not healed it becomes a very definite pain and can amount to torture, and it requires torture to make many of us think.

Mr. Crichton Miller in his book, " The New Psychology and the Preacher," says with justice : " Christianity as presented to the masses for many centuries has emphatically discouraged thinking." And yet it is doubtful whether there can be any true religion without thought, only we must not confuse thought with book-learning —there are many very learned people who scarcely ever think at all.

True thought is an effort to find the meaning of things and it is always pain that drives us to it, whether it be that we find something wrong with the motor-car in which we drive or in the universe in which we live, it is a pain in the mind that makes us think about it. It may make us swear about it, grow bitter, lose our tempers and take to violence : all these are substitutes for thought.

Constantly men are tempted to turn problems into battles and so escape the cross of thought. It is a fatal thing to do yet we are constantly doing it both in our politics and in our religion. We divide the Body of Christ into parties and sects and make up for our sloth in thinking by our loyalty in strife. And we do the same in politics, displaying a zeal which is not according to knowledge. But if we would live we cannot escape the necessity of thinking about life.

True life only begins when a man is troubled about life, troubled as to what it means. The difference between a man and an animal is just that capacity for being troubled. Animals, despite their sufferings, appear to be content ; man, despite his blessings and his supremacy over all animals, is perpetually in discontent. That is why people who have not yet begun to live in any human sense of that word appear often to be happier than the saints ; they have not begun to wonder, to ask questions and to be sad, they are content to muddle through anyhow. That really means that they are not yet awake ; the human head, the human heart and the human soul are still asleep, and there will be for them no awaking until they are troubled.

All triumph is born of tragedy. The triumph of the scientist and the triumph of the saint are both born from the trouble of the mind. John Bunyan, brooding over the problem of his soul, and Johann Kepler, brooding over the problem of the stars, are alike in this, they are troubled in mind, and the only relief that can come to them must come of a moment of vision ; there must come to both, there did come to both, the moment when they cried, " I see." One saw the Cross, the other saw the law of gravity, and the result of both visions was the coming of peace. The triumphant moment in the life of the scientist is the moment when he conceives his great hypothesis which gives meaning to a large number of apparently disconnected and disordered facts over which he has been brooding with a troubled mind. The triumphant moment of the saint is the moment of his conversion when he sees in His Lord the meaning of the disconnected and disorderly experiences which go to make up human life. And when they have passed through their moment of vision there remains for both the great task of implicit obedience to that which they have seen ; for the scientist this means the testing of his hypothesis, for the saint, the living of his faith.

The Christian faith is the great religious hypothesis, in it the Christian sees the meaning of life. The scientific hypothesis eases the pain of the mind that is always asking as it looks at and wonders about this strange universe : " How did it come to be ? " the religious hypothesis eases the pain in the mind that as it looks upon the universe and wonders is always asking: Why did it come to be.

Science does not, and does not profess to tell us anything about the Why of the world, about its purpose, about its ultimate meaning, it only deals with the How of it—how it grew, how it lives, how it works. Our knowledge of how it grew and lives and works is infinitely greater than that of our forefathers, but apart from religion we are not an inch nearer to answering the question which is even greater torture to the mind, as to Why it grew and lives and works as it does. All the wonderful knowledge of the How of the universe only makes us cry out more earnestly Why? Why should things be so? What is the meaning of the universe and the end of it all?

In Christ born in Bethlehem, crucified on Calvary, conquering death, rising again, there is revealed to us the meaning of life in terms of perfect personality, the only terms which could be ultimately satisfactory. The great faith says that the meaning of the vast and terrible process of evolution is God suffering in and through man to bring him to glory. Evolution is ascension through sacrifice to perfection.

When I stand feeling like a pigmy beneath the silent stars of a summer night, looking up at the mountains, listening to the sea, with the cry of the tortured ages of human history in my ears and the knowledge of the creative eons in my mind, and ask as I am bound to ask, Why? there is no voice that answers except the voice of the Son of Man who died and rose again. Once I hear that Voice with the ears that can really hear, the pain in my mind begins to pass into peace.

There is pain still, there are problems that baffle, mysteries that are not yet cleared up, but it is no longer a hopeless trouble, I become sure that faith in Christ accepted by the intellect will solve for me all problems in the world and out of it at last. So the Good Shepherd makes me to lie down in green pastures and leads me beside the still waters, sets me free to think in peace. But there is not only a hunger of the head, there is a hunger of the heart, nor can the two be separated as easily as men suppose. The head will not cease from hungering until the heart is satisfied.

There is no more barren form of idolatry than the worship of the intellect. It is essentially idolatry, for an idol is something that claims a power apart from God which it cannot possess. Man has triumphed over nature by means of what he calls " scientific thinking," that is, thinking as far as possible divorced from feeling. He has schooled himself to crush out all emotion and endeavoured to see things as they are and not as he wants them to be. And this has led him to the belief that feeling and thought are in some way essentially opposed and that the only way to think straight is to destroy feeling.

Now it is possible to do this to a certain extent when we are thinking about abstract subjects which have no emotional content of their own. It is possible to think about a question of mathematics apparently without any emotion whatever, and all the scientific knowledge by which we have gained supremacy over nature is abstract. Biology and chemistry are really just as abstract as mathematics. But because we can think impartially and without feeling upon abstract subjects that does not mean that we can do the same with what one calls " live issues." The man who imagines that he can think without feeling upon any question that involves his pride, his pocket, his country, his family, is simply deceiving himself. These " live issues " by their very nature involve feeling, and all that the clever man does who professes to be scientific and impartial about them, is to use his intellect to discover elaborate and wholly artificial reasons for doing what his impulses drive him to do.

The heart is really stronger than the head in every one of us whenever it comes to things that really matter, and the stronger our heads are the more astounding and ultimately unreasonable are the means which the heart will use to satisfy itself. Clever devils, men whose heads are clear and whose hearts are foul, are the curse of the world. In every department of life we suffer from them, it is they that prolong the tortures of the people. In the last issue it is what you love that makes you what you are, and what you are that determines actually the worth or worse than worthlessness of what you think.

A really clever man or woman finds it fatally easy not only to deceive others but to deceive themselves, and justify conduct in themselves which is in reality utterly unjustifiable. Conscious hypocrites are rarer than people suppose, for much that the world calls hypocrisy is the honest strife of very imperfect men, but unconscious hypocrisy is much commoner than people suppose, and the very cleverest men and women are often the victims of it. Their mental powers enable them to impose their own mischevious imaginations upon more simple people and upon themselves. It is never the fool who really wrecks and ruins the family or the nation, it is the able man who has never found the true meaning of life and is still trying to build the world about himself as centre; the man whose hunger of the heart is still unsatisfied and who has not found the great love.

The heart is really the master whether you like it or not, and if the master be wrong the servants can but do his will.   If the light that is within them be darkness, how great is that darkness.

The supreme question for us all is, What do you want ?   What do you love ? and it is here that the Good Shepherd comes in to minister to our necessity, our necessity let us repeat, comes in to give us not luxuries and extras, but comes in to give us what we must have. If we pretend that we can do without it we do but deceive ourselves.   If we do not love Beauty, Truth and Goodness as it is in Christ Jesus we will love some beauty, truth and goodness of our own, some person or reality.   If we will not have Jesus for our God then we must either find a better one or serve a worse. If we pretend that we have not got one we are merely fooling ourselves.   Atheism is not a creed, it is a nervous disease, it means life without anything to live for, and that is hell.

When a man tells me that he has no religion I simply take it that he is talking nonsense and proceed to find out what his religion is, what it is that gives life meaning to him.   I may of course discover that life really has no meaning for him at all, and in that case I begin to be anxious about his sanity, and if he comes to me for advice, immediately consider sending him to a doctor. But of course what one generally discovers is that the man or woman has a god but a poor one, and because he has a poor god he is a poor person and is still in want, not knowing what he wants but unhappy till he gets it.

To the making of gods apart from Jesus there is no end, and most of them are devils.   If a man lives for anything that Jesus could not bless it is impossible it could be any use to himself or to the world.   None of us, of course, have seen all that Christ means and is, but most of us live on the fragment of it that we have seen and our lives are worth what we have seen of Him and nothing more. The life that is lived for something altogether outside of Him, such as the lust of the eye or the pride of life, is just waste of time which is the most awful thing in the world, and yet it is in waste of time that the world is mainly engaged. As the late Mr. Clutton Brock puts it : " Our whole society now spends its superfluous energies in activities which would seem to it insane if it were not so used to them, and the causes of which it does not even attempt to understand. We are in the dangerous state of an individual who is controlled in the main by his unconscious I, by desires of which he is unaware, and who finds reasons for his behaviour which are never the true reasons. Consider for instance the energy and money we spend on games and on watching them, on contests between prize fighters, on horse racing and all kinds of gambling, on the means of rushing from place to place, and on substitutes for art, such as the cinema. We do not know why we do these things, we cannot analyse or account for the pleasures we get from them, we cannot even say whether the feeling aroused by them is pleasure ; all we know is that we are like Blake's figure of a child which stretches out its hand and cries, ' I want, I want.' Without knowing what our wants are we spend more and more money in satisfying them and always the process becomes more and more expensive, being indeed valued because of its expense."

We are wasting money, that is wasting energy—for money is just a symbol of energy, our own or other peoples—and wasting time because we do not know what we want, because we have not found our God, and until we can cry, " I believe in God and I know Him in whom I have believed," we shall continue not to live but merely to waste life.

He maketh me to lie down in green pastures

The crucial question for the man who denies that Christ is divine is to decide what is or who is, for man lives for the divine, or to put it another way, his divinity is what he lives for, and he must live for something or somebody, and if not for Christ then for whom? For his country, you say. What do you mean by that? What does he want for his country? that it should be great, powerful and rich above all others? There are many who live for that and they are tearing God's world into pieces. For his family, you say. What does he want for his family? that it should be prosperous, comfortable and independent? There are thousands who live for that and they are tearing God's world into pieces. For humanity, you say. What does he want for humanity? that it should be comfortable, rich, free from sorrow and from pain? There are some few who live for that and they are breaking their hearts and pursuing an empty dream; for any one or all who are working for these ends that they may be what Christ could bless, then is he touching the garment of reality and life begins. But however you work it there is no escape from the necessity of Christ. There is only one way out, that is that you should find someone better, someone more beautiful than He. Apart from that you must wander in the wilderness of wasting time, seeking an unknown and unknowable promised land. Because I find in Him the supremely worthy object of my love, therefore He makes me to lie down in green pastures and leads me beside the still waters and satisfies the hunger of my heart.

But lastly, there is not only hunger of the head and hunger of the heart, there is hunger of the soul. When I have seen the truth as it is in Jesus, and seen Beauty as it is blessed by Him, straightway am I brought into bitter conflict with myself and with the world. I am brought face to face with the utter mystery, the mystery of ugliness and evil. I find it everywhere in myself and in the world, and having seen the meaning of both in Him it becomes intolerable. In proportion to the clearness of my vision there arises in me a rage to destroy it, to destroy ugliness and evil right out of the world, and that is the test of my vision. No one who had really seen the meaning of life could henceforth tolerate evil.

Christ does not explain, there is no explanation of it, it can no more be explained than the writings of a lunatic. The essence of it is irrational. There is only one way of solving the problem of evil, and that is destroying it, and here you and I are brought face to face with our extremist need, the need of power to destroy evil and ugliness in ourselves and in the world. If the Good Shepherd forsook us here all our gain would be turned to loss and all our joy to sorrow, He would but open the doors of heaven that we might look inside and then slam them in our face bidding us begone.

Just so far as you can tolerate the injustice, the cruelty, the dirt and degradation that is in the world, just so sure can you be that you have not seen Him. The test and hall mark of the vision is the strength of your rebellion against it. The greatest reproach of the churches is that they have so long tolerated and compromised with evil in the world. If you can really rest content while men and women sleep six and seven in a bedroom, as they do in North Kensington, for I have seen them, and in Birmingham, and even in some villages ; if you can rest content while men are overworked and under-paid ; if you can tolerate the waste and cruelty of war, the degradation of prostitution, you have not seen Him, you have not found your God, you are still not living but wasting life.

He maketh me to lie down in green pastures

The Good Shepherd intensifies to the point of torture the hunger of the soul until it becomes a passion in man to make the world in which he lives as beautiful and as good as he perceives that it is meant to be ; He intensifies the hunger to the point of torture that He may satisfy it by the gift of communion with Himself and the moral power that springs from that communion.

I Believe !

Is God Love or is He brute Force. Is Christianity true or is it a tissue of dangerous sentimentality. Can it save or will it ruin the world ? If it is false, then let us cast it aside before it is too late. He will kill you, that old self-satisfied you, unless you kill Him. You see it must be one thing or the other. It is either a vision of reality or mirage that torments us travellers in the desert, and tempts us to our doom. Do you believe that the way of reason, self-sacrifice, service, and love is the way of life for you and all mankind ? Do you dare to rise and walk on it ? Do you believe, knowing the risks you run, and all you must give up, that Jesus was the Incarnate Word and that life is a new Birth—a Crucifixion, a Resurrection, and an Ascension ? Will you risk a real Good Friday to win an Easter Day ?

Lord, I believe, help Thou mine unbelief. I look upon the world and I see a Baby on a Mother's Breast, a Body broken on a cross, an empty tomb with a great stone rolled away, and one like unto the Son of Man with wounded Hands outstretched to bless ascending to His glory, and I believe that right at the heart of the ultimate reality there was in the beginning, is now, and ever shall be a Person expressing a rational purpose that I can in some measure understand. I believe that this Person was, is, and ever shall be with God, and indeed is God, though it is nearer the Truth to say " with God " because the Father is greater than He. I believe

I Believe !

that through this Person all things came into being, and that apart from Him—not a single thing came into being which is of the nature of reality. In Him are the eternal sources of life, and life became light in men, and the light shines in the darkness and the darkness cannot swallow it up. I believe that this Person took upon Him our human nature, and lived a human life, and that men beheld, and can now behold His glory—which is the glory of the only perfect expression of that Love which is the ultimate and absolute reality of all things.

Charity

THERE is no word in the English language which has had a stranger and more tragic history than the word charity. It once was the queen of all the words, the name of God Himself, but it has gradually come down in the world, until it has in our days become an outcast going from door to door begging for leave to live. Nobody wants and everybody suspects charity. Give us justice not charity is the cry of the poor; this is business not charity is the sneer of the practical man.

How has it come to pass that this word which stood so high when we first got our English Bible has fallen so low in modern times. Originally it was used as the name for the very highest and finest kind of Love. God knows we need a name, a special name, for that perfect Love to-day as badly as we ever did. We over-work the word Love, we use it for everything, for things in the depths of hell, and things in the heights of heaven. We call the brutal and cruel sex passion which is the main theme of the cinema thrill, the animal attraction between man and woman, which torments and drives them to torture one another, and is the most savage, untamed, and tyrannical impulse of human nature, we call that Love. The exploitation of that crude passion is one of the most paying propositions on the market to-day, if you know how to appeal to it, excite, and stimulate it. You can make thousands where honest labour will yield but poor returns. We call it Love, and the confusion of the names is the sign of our confusion of what the names represent. God is Love, and a three times divorced cinema actor is the perfect Lover, and heaven gets mixed up with hell. We call the tolerance of other people's faults and the willingness to live and let live, the tottering and perpetually wobbling basis of our ordinary social intercourse, what is properly called good nature, we call that Love too. And when we seek a name for the Love which burns in the heart of the finest men and women in the world, the passion to serve and save their fellow men, we can find no other, and we call it Love.

But it is a bad business this mixing up of God and the devil. The Greeks were more sensible. They had two different words. Crude sex passion they called " eros," and they knew it was a savage thing. Good nature they called " philia," and when the Christian saints wanted to find a name for the highest kind of Love, the generous desire to suffer for and help the human race, they invented a new word altogether, and called it " agape," and it was that word which the translators of our New Testament rendered as " charity." Charity therefore really means the desire to make men, the finest kind of men and women, and the willingness to sacrifice one's own interest and pleasure to do it. It is that desire which ought to be the driving force behind all business, all industry, and all politics.

It may sound mad to say that the House of Commons ought to be a charitable institution, but if we use the words accurately, it ought to be just that and nothing else. If the passion behind politics is anything lower or less than the desire to foster and create in our country the highest and finest kind of life, and there is not in the hearts of politicians and statesmen a willingness to spend and be spent for that great end, then politics have no real meaning, and are just a hollow sham. It may sound even madder to say that any great industry ought to be a charitable institution, but it is true. Unless the desire to create and sustain in the people the best and finest kind of life is working in every industry, industry cannot fulfil its purpose. The root reason why both our politics and our industries are in a state of chaos is that they are driven, in the main, by lower and more primitive desires, which being in a perpetual state of conflict in the hearts of men, produce conflict in the society they create. Real Charity is the only power that can lift the world out of chaos and build an order of society worthy of reasonable men. We must cease to degrade the word, or we shall continue to degrade that high and splendid desire for which it stands. I want to make live, strong men, healthy in body, and clear in mind, pure women, and jolly children with sunshine in their eyes. I want that, and I work for it, and only so far as my work, or anyone else's has that desire behind it, has it any constructive value for the world.

We call it charity when men gave away what they did not want themselves in order to patch up evils and ameliorate bad conditions which their greed, slackness, or stupidity have helped to create. This is not charity, and it is blasphemy to call it by that splendid name. We call it charity when we give a poor devil half a crown to get shut of him and rid ourselves of the sight of his misery, that is blasphemy too. Real charity is not easy, it is always hard, it means that we must be ready to take time, trouble, and infinite pains to create life. The business man who seeks to give good value for money, who prides himself on his fellow workers in the business, and whose aim is to see that by efficiency, and energy his business produces and sustains fine life, he is the

charitable man.   Our faith is that God is Charity—that
His charity is so great that He spares Himself no suffer-
ing and no agony in order to create in the world fine life.
We are meet to be like Him.

Go and do thou likewise

OF all the stories told by the Nazarene there is no one that has held the human imagination more powerfully than the story of the Good Samaritan, the picture of the poor fellow lying wounded and bleeding on the road from Jerusalem to Jericho. There is the exquisite character touch of the one man who hurries by in deadly fear without even looking at him, and the other who, while he goes to the length of stopping to see what's up and half wanting to help, starts thinking of himself, and, remembering that there might be other thieves knocking around, immediately turns away with terror in his face and pelts down the road as fast as his legs will carry him so as to get to Jericho before dark. And finally, the decent old Samaritan on his donkey coming along in the gloaming and doing the necessary kindness, despite the fact that the man was a Jew and he was a Samaritan, and the Jews felt towards the Samaritans very much what the English felt for the Germans immediately after the sinking of the *Lusitania*.

It is a wonderful picture drawn by a master hand and by one who, as S. John says, knew men and needed not that any should tell Him what was in men. And there is no human conscience not completely dead, that does not answer, for a moment at any rate, to the command " Go and do thou likewise." Many would say in fact that in this command, honestly and earnestly obeyed, lies all that really matters about the Christian faith.

But if you set out to obey it in earnest you begin to find that it isn't as easy as it looks, this Good Samaritan business.

To start with, what you find in life is that there isn't only one road from Jerusalem to Jericho that is infested by thieves. Men can go to Jericho in all sorts of ways and women too, and this old world of ours is plagued with an infinite variety of sharks going around seeking what they can pick up. The first problem that hits the man who sets out to be a good Samaritan is just the problem of numbers.

You see, the Good Samaritan in the story was lucky, he only struck one man that had been knocked out, and he had all that was necessary—a donkey, some oil and wine, and twopence. But when I go out on that tack I don't find one man, I find processions of them, and I have not got all that is necessary. If I am to do it properly I seem to need a bottomless pocket, infinite wisdom, a fleet of motor-cars and a general hospital, and even that would not be enough, because an enormous number of these poor devils that lie beside the roads to Jericho have not merely been knocked about bodily, they have lost their characters, they have lost their power of will, they are without hope in the world and without faith in themselves or in anything else. And it's when you get up against a proposition like that that you begin to realise your own limitations and to feel the need of some power greater than yourself. Giving money away is a ticklish business and as likely to do harm as good, and anyhow, when you get a fellow who has lost himself so to speak, money is no good at all.

The truth is that playing the Good Samaritan if you do it square and honest, drives you back to the necessity of a Saviour and of a Gospel of salvation. If there is no such thing as the Love of God and His redeeming

Power, the endeavour to play the Good Samaritan on the million roads that in this world lead downward from Jerusalem to Jericho would break the heart of the bravest and burst the brain of the cleverest that ever lived on earth. I guess that's partly what the Gospel story means. There was once One who tried to play Good Samaritan to us all, and He lay in a garden and cried in pain and broke out into bloody sweat.

And there is another side to it. It was all right for the Good Samaritan in the story picking up the chap by the road side, but he did not own the road ; if he had owned the road, his duty would have been to get it cleared of thieves, and not to keep trotting along with a donkey picking up men that had been knocked out.

And that brings you up with a bump against the whole social problem, because you and I are part owners at any rate of these roads to Jericho that are infested by sharks and thieves, and it doesn't do for us to think that our duty ends in helping to supply endless charitable funds, and financing innumerable societies to save the under-dog. We cannot stop short of an earnest endeavour to clear out the thieves, and so to strengthen the travellers on the road that they may be able to defend themselves against those we cannot clear out.

And that is the double way the Good Samaritan story hits me. First of all, that if I am to be any good I need to look after my own soul, I need God, I want to have an extra store of faith and hope, of vigour and vitality with which to inspire and uplift those who fall out by the way. Men are always thinking of a parson as a pious sort of bloke who goes about holding up his hands in horror and cursing people for their sins. But that's not the way I look at it at all. My job really is doctoring people that doctors are no good to, and helping people that nothing on earth but only God can help, and striving all I know to give people faith and hope and power to be happy. There are more sins committed because men and women are bored and miserable and hopeless than for any other cause whatsoever, and if by preaching or teaching or talking or just by being friends with them I can give them faith and hope and the Love of God, then I am doing my job. And it isn't only a parson's job, it is the job of every man and woman in the world so far as they can do it. A parson has to try and do it for lots of people—everyone can do it for some.

It's right enough that if you really go and do likewise you won't be far from the Kingdom of God, but it's no easy task, and if you set about it honestly you will be on your knees in a fortnight asking God for help. If that is not true, I am a Dutchman. People are always saying to me, " I need not go to Church and I need not say any prayers, I can be perfectly good without either " —if you mean by being good, not running away with your neighbour's wife, paying your debts and speaking the truth more or less—you may manage all right—but not if you mean by being good the Good Samaritan touch. If you are going to do that you must have a spring-cleaning inside and you must go on seeking hope in the hopeless, power to love the unlovely, to see beauty in the unbeautiful and give strength to the weak and wobbly, or you will inevitably find yourself unequal to the task. When a man comes in and sits down before you and tells you that he has made a complete muddle of his life and has nothing left to live for and care for in the world and might as well go to the devil quick, you may be as rich as Crœsus and as clever as Winston Churchill, but he would have you beat to the wide unless you had something more.

Jesus of Nazareth knew what He was about, and before He said to this fellow who was trying to catch him out and to whom he told the immortal story " Go and do thou likewise," He told him solemnly, " The first and greatest commandment is, Thou shalt love the Lord thy God with all thy heart, with all thy soul, with all thy mind and with all thy strength, and then comes the second, Thou shalt love thy neighbour as thyself."

A man has never been up against ultimate reality until he has stood beside a fellow man knocked out on the road down to Jericho and, looking at him, realised with horror that he had no donkey, no wine or oil, and not a sou to bless himself with, and nothing to give but himself. Then it is that a man asks " What am I worth ? " and cries on his God for help. I have been there many a time and have known, God help me, that I am not worth much.

Treasure upon Earth

" LAY not up for yourselves treasure upon earth where moth and rust doth corrupt, and where thieves break through and steal : but lay up for yourselves treasure in heaven, where neither moth nor rust doth corrupt and where thieves do not break through and steal ; for where your treasure is, there will your heart be also." That is one of the Master's sayings that brings you up against big things with a bump.

It seems at first sight a hard saying, as though he were telling us that this world is no good except as a preparation for the next. Nothing in this world lasts. It all passes away, and therefore if your heart be set upon it, all you will get in the end will be a broken heart. Even if your treasures be stored in a big sound Bank and escape the moth and the rust, Death, the great thief, will break through at last and steal them all away. There is deep truth in that. It is hard to believe that the old lady in the corner, huddled over the fire, twisted with rheumatism, and gasping for breath was once the girl with snow-white arms and soft brown eyes whose picture smiles down at you from over the mantelpiece. Once when she walked down the way of the world men turned to look and look again, they felt the blood run faster in their veins, and one man at least was fired to suffer, and to labour, and for her sweet sake to do what this world counts great things. Now he is dead and she is dying. The great thief stands behind her biding his time but ready for the end. It was hard to believe as we stood by his bed that the shrivelled old fellow, fed like a child by a kindly nurse, had once swayed thousands by his words, made history by his wisdom, and led men into battle like a God. Yet so it was. I remember he turned his face to the window, opened his mouth as though to speak, smiled, struggled, and was gone.

Does that mean that her beauty and his work were no good ? Were they of no value in themselves, only made like children's toys to be broken or put away with other childish things ? Did they serve no higher purpose than to pass the time, and perhaps to help in some small way, as good toys do, to train just those two souls for a fuller future life ? Is this world and our life upon this earth only a childish game which the great God watches with a smile as we watch our children when they build with their toy bricks the castles that at bed-time must be swept away ? Often the teaching of the Christ has been interpreted as meaning that. The beauty of women, and the ordinary work of men and women in the world have been regarded by Christian teachers as of little or no ultimate value. The highest life it was supposed was led by those who forsook this world, and devoted themselves to prayer, and constant preparation for the next. Because of the frailty of human nature it was recognised that all men and women could not do this, and so love, marriage, manual labour, and secular learning were tolerated, but not valued as of any lasting worth. The study of nature and of nature's laws was discouraged as waste of time. A man or woman would be no more fit for heaven because they had studied and partly understood the nature of the earth. The best way of living therefore was to remember, and constantly prepare for death.

Against this way of living and of looking at life there

has in these latter days been a great world-wide revolt. Men everywhere have thrown off the tyranny of the next world, and have set themselves to the perfecting of this. The highest honours are no longer paid to those who forsake the earth, and the treasures of it, to the saints and men of prayer, but to the scientists, artists, statesmen and reformers, captains of industry, and the like, the men of affairs who set themselves with energy, wisdom, and enterprise to increase and improve the treasure upon earth. Does this mean that we have thrown over the teaching of the Christ, and deliberately disobeyed His command. Are we really turned pagan again ? Is all our boasted progress, scientific advance, and prosperity mere vanity and folly ? Are we only laying up for ourselves treasure upon earth which the moth and rust of time must corrupt, and the great thief at last break through to steal " when all the labour of the ages, all the devotion, all the noonday brightness of the human genius come to their destiny of extinction in the vast death of the solar system, when the whole temple of man's achievement must inevitably be buried beneath the debris of a universe in ruins." Shall we come to the rich fool's end at the last and hear God's voice saying " Thou fool, this night shall thy soul be required of thee."

There are some good men in the world who think that. They believe the world is changing for the worse and not the better, and that all the hurry and rush of our modern life is getting us nowhere. But I think they are wrong. I think they are wrong because they fail to recognize the truth that while God's heaven exists and has existed from all eternity, man's heaven is something that must be made, and is being made by man under the inspiration, help, and guidance of God. They think of heaven as a Holy City, a new Jerusalem, already finished and completely ready for the human race into which those who are fit will pass at death, and find there nothing to do. But that I believe is a wrong and unworthy thought. The new Jerusalem is still being built. It is the result of all the fine and honest work, all the tireless searching after truth, all the artistic creation of beauty which God's children have accomplished on the earth. There, as here, we shall inherit the labour of our fathers, and it will be our joy to carry it on to its completion. We shall find built into the life of that city all the decent honest work and thinking we have by God been called to do in the sunshine and the shadow of our sojourn here, and shall know that our labour is not vain in the Lord. If indeed we do bad work, and think mean thoughts of life ; if we labour only for our lower selves with no desire of service to God or to mankind ; if we scamp the job to make it pay, and set out to make money and not men, then we do lay up for ourselves treasure upon earth and nowhere else, and however successful we may be the sooner the moth and the rust get busy the better, and thieves can get no swag, but trash.

But it was not so with them, these two of whom I think. She was a woman and he was a man of the world in the best sense. But there was something of eternal worth in the gay and gallant beauty of the maid. She was no plaster saint. She flirted a bit in her time, and evil tongues were busy round her once. But they were wrong. The evil was in them, not her. She never let men down. She was not out for scalps. She would not stoop to sell herself. She took some time to choose her mate. Where many offer it is often hard to choose, and many brave men wanted her. But when she chose she stuck through thick and thin. She knew her own mind and was right.

Treasure upon Earth

How many loved your moments of glad grace,
And loved your beauty with love false and true ;
But one man loved the pilgrim soul in you,
And loved the sorrows of your changing face.

He was not an easy man to live with, but she knew his worth. She never made a slave of him or tied him to her apron strings. She gave him freely to the world, bore his babes, and fired him to work. And he did good work. He was not perfect. He had his faults, a temper like a tornado and a bitter tongue. But he did good work. He worked till he was tired out, and played on still when the game seemed all but up. It was in the world, very much in the world, and for the world they worked, these two, and yet I believe that the treasure they laid up was not only on the earth. Rust cannot touch her real beauty, nor thieves the wealth he made, for there was genuine love in them both, and where Love is there is heaven, where neither moth nor rust doth corrupt and where even the great thief cannot break through to steal.

If there had been no Christmas

IF Jesus had not lived what would the world be like to-day? "It could not be much worse than it is," I hear the cynic say with a sneer. I wonder. It is our human way to take good things for granted and cry out against the evil that maims and mars our lives. To some extent perhaps it is inevitable that we should do this. The roots of man's divinity are in his discontent. We must take the earth for granted that we may stand and turn our faces to the sky. What use for us to ask ourselves what might have been had earth been other than it is?

And yet I have often asked myself that very question. I am told, with sound evidence to back the statement, that the fourth Glacial Age reached its bitterest climax about fifty thousand years ago, and that it was amidst the snows of that long universal winter of the world that the first man-like beings lived upon our planet, and looked with frightened eyes upon the huge ungainly mammoth whose monstrous bones are left to tell the tale. When I have been reading of those far-off times, and as I ponder over the record of the rocks trying to picture to myself what it must have been like to live in those days when the wintry death of the Great Ice Age crept southward over the earth, when the Arctic Musk and the Reindeer herds roamed round Oxford Street and Piccadilly, the years when there was no spring, I have often laid down my book and asked myself, with a kind of awe and wonder in my inmost soul, " What if there had been no spring? What if the ice had never broken, and the white snow never ceased to fall? "

" Absurd," you say. Maybe. Perhaps all questions as to what might have been are absurd. The past is past and our only concern with it is to use it as a foundation for the future. And yet to think upon what might have been may help us to appreciate what is. To picture to ourselves that endless winter may help us to see with clearer eyes the splendour of God's spring. The connection between Christmas and the end of the great world winter is perhaps closer than anyone ignorant of history would suppose. Why is December 25th kept as Christmas Day? Why does it come in the very depth of winter? We do not really know the exact date of Christ's Birth. December 25th was not fixed as the Birthday Festival of Christ until three hundred years after He died. It was then settled not because December 25th was known to be the true date of His Birth but because it was the day of the heathen midwinter festival. Traces of that heathen festival are still with us. The burning of the Yule log goes back to days long, long before the Christ, and so do Christmas trees. Behind the ancient winter festival there lay the dread that in the depth of some bleak winter the sun might really die, bleeding its life out in the flames of one last awful sunset across the western sky. That primitive dread that made the ancients pile the Yule logs up to warm the sun lest it die in winter's grip was a racial memory of the long world winter their fathers had endured.

The more we know of the human mind the more reason we have for believing that the roots of our common customs strike down into the depths of an unconsciously remembered past. The instinct that made the early

The New Man in Christ

Christians keep the Festival of Christ's Birth upon midwinter day was the result of a very vivid experience. They felt that the coming of Christ into the world had been like the return of the sun, the winter of the world's soul was over and the spring had come. The contrast between the darkness before Him and the Light which He brought was to them a glaring and startling contrast because the memory of the darkness was still fresh, and the remains of it were still with them. It is less glaring to us because Christ has been at work for many years, and the memory of the darkness has faded into the dim background of our minds. We cannot easily recall it. It is only by using the written and recorded memory of history that we can make the darkness real to ourselves. The only word which would serve to convey any idea of the darkness from which the early Christians felt that Christ had saved them would be " devilry." There has existed in the world a depth of sinister, callous, coldblooded, cruel wickedness which we rarely meet with to-day, but it was common and powerful in the ancient world. If you want to get back into that atmosphere you must study the history of superstition, and remember that the ancient world was sunk in superstition. It is terrible reading. Truth is stranger than fiction, and the mind reels and is shocked by these records of the foul, filthy, cruel things men have believed, and the ghastly deeds that have been done because of those beliefs.

When I hear men say that the world is no better than it was I wonder at their ignorance. They do not know what devilry means. They take Christ for granted, and live in a rational world where men and women are no longer afraid, a world from which the terror of the unknown and the secret slavery of superstitious fear has been banished after centuries of spiritual warfare.

If there had been no Christmas

Christianity has to a large extent become common sense. Taught by Christ we assume that the world we live in is a friendly place and that the worst we have to fear is death. But that assumption, and the inner freedom from fear which springs from it, are the result of centuries of teaching the great Truth that God is Love. Slowly and painfully against awful and mysterious odds that truth has made its way setting men free from fear, and from the cruelty that fear inevitably breeds. The battle is not over yet, for superstition may return in a different form. If men cast Christ aside and come to believe that the world is a vast, soulless, unreasoning machine with nothing behind it but a mechanical fate which makes murderous wars inevitable and peace impossible. If they come to believe that there is nothing and no one in the universe greater and better than man and that man himself is nothing but an animal with a bigger brain, then the old fear may return, and darkness fall on the earth again. As I read some of our ultra modern teaching with its contempt for God and Man, its cynical jeering at our highest hopes, its relentless analysis of our deepest feelings which reduces soul to sense, religion to sex, and all hope of heaven to a foolish dream, I feel the ancient fear return.

Men put their trust in science, but a soulless and unloving science is the most sinister superstition that has ever threatened to destroy the sanity of man. Science controlled by Faith and Love may lead us to the Kingdom of God, but Science controlled by cynical and unbelieving intelligence will lead us back into the dark again. The ancient evil is not dead, the devils in the soul of man are subject to, but have not been slain by, Christ. The Mystery of iniquity is still a reality. I have seen it in the days when I walked in the valley of destruction and often rubbed elbows with death. Out of the night we came, and back to the night we may return if we lose our vision of the light of the world. We may, we do continually, outgrow and leave behind the dogmatic expressions of the Truth of Christ, but we cannot leave behind the Truth itself unless we turn our faces from the light and move back to the darkness whence we came. If there had been no Christmas then this world would have been a different world, as different as it would have been if in those distant days the ice had never broken and the white snow never ceased to fall. If there had been no Christmas the night of evil superstition might still be on the earth and the ancient devils might be Kings not captives bound with chains.

> Christ that was born on Christmas Day,
> Laid on the world His two small hands,
> Lifting it worlds and worlds away
> Up to the level of Love's demands.

> And those Hands hold though pierced with nails
> They hold on still in power and pain,
> And they shall hold till Satan fails
> And Love comes to His own to reign.

God Save the King

I HAVE just been reading a life of Benjamin Disraeli. It is a fascinating story. I suppose that of all forms of writing biography must be the most difficult, and the greater the man the greater the difficulty. This biography is a good one. I lay it down with the satisfied feeling that I really know something of the man, and understand how he came to be what he was, and to do what he did. Of course there is a mystery about all great men, a mystery which no biographer can hope entirely to explain. There are always questions to which there can never be any answers.

The four Gospels are a case in point. They are in one way masterpieces of biography. Here is a perfect portrait drawn with a direct simplicity of strong clear lines which all the waters of two thousand years have not been able to wash out. Across the ages their cry and their challenge may still ring clear : Ecce Homo ! Behold the Man. But what an enormous number of questions they leave unanswered and unanswerable. One would give much for a contemporary biography of the Son of Man written in the fuller modern style. If only someone could with authority break the silence of those first thirty years, and give us an authentic picture of the Home at Nazareth. We know little or nothing about it. After the Christmas stories with their atmosphere of unearthly beauty the silence is complete and unbroken except for the incident of the Doctors in the temple. And that incident asks more questions than it answers. That very human and natural mother's question, " Son, why hast thou dealt thus with us, behold Thy father and I have sought thee sorrowing," and the very odd and incomprehensible reply, " How is it that ye sought me ? Wist ye not that I must be about my Father's business," or " in my Father's house," as it ought possibly to be translated. Wouldn't you love to know what His mother said next, and what Joseph thought about it ?

I have known what it means for a father to seek a lost child and I feel that for his mother's sake, if not for my own, I would have had a good deal to say. The Boy was twelve years old and should have thought about his mother's distress. If these two parents said nothing further they were certainly wonderful and they may have been wonderfully wise. For the man or woman who always deals wisely with a growing child is the wisest person in the world. I doubt if there is anything more difficult to be wise about than our treatment of our children as they grow up. As they develop minds, interests, and wills of their own a great gulf seems to grow up between us and them, a gulf which both we and they find it difficult to bridge. Perhaps the wisest of us do not try to bridge it although the temptation to do so is as strong as Love itself. It is this almost inevitable gulf between the generations, and the tension it creates, which makes the building of a good and happy home so difficult a task that it calls for the very best we have in us, for wisdom, for patience, for sacrifice, and self-control. A good home is not a gift but an achievement, and a very difficult achievement too.

Just because history is so completely silent about the home at Nazareth imagination has been busy with it. Because fact fails us fiction has been made to take its

place. We have idealised it freely, and made of it a
supernaturally perfect thing, a perfect mother, a perfect
father, and the perfect child. But fiction utterly
divorced from fact is a dangerous thing, and there is a
danger in this. We may be so anxious to make it
perfect that we make it impossible. It may become unnatural instead of supernatural. Inhuman rather than
superhuman. The picture then loses its power and
becomes repulsive. It has the sickening sweetness of
the purely sentimental. It is I think precisely that
which has happened to our picture of Christ's home. It
has ceased to be good because it has become goody
goody. And yet silent as the Gospel stories are upon
the thirty years they do not supply us with evidence
sufficient to protect us from that. There is the strange
incident recorded in S. Mark, in which we are told that
on one occasion his friends and family, including his
mother, went out to lay hold upon him because they
thought he was mad. His mother thought he was mad.
There is surely food for thought in that. There is the
curious reply made to those who told him that his mother
and brothers were seeking him. He looked round upon
those who sat listening to his teaching and said, " Who
are my mother and my brethren. Those who do the
will of God are my father and my mother, my sisters,
and my brothers." There is also the passage in S. John
which records something very like a dispute between
Jesus and his brothers, and gives as a reason for it that
" even his brethren believed not on him."

There is sufficient indication of the reality here to
give us ground for rejecting the sentimental, too easily
perfect, picture of that home life. And we are well rid
of it. No idea is more false or more dangerous than the
all too common idea that happy homes are easily made,
that people are either happily or unhappily married, and

can do very little about it themselves either way because it depends upon their temperaments, or the notion that children must naturally and easily love and respect their parents simply because they are parents. The sentimentalism which attempts to ignore as though they did not exist the very real difficulties which must be faced in the making of a home, is disastrous because it leads people to imagine that marriage ought to be a picnic or a paradise, and that a home can be made without wisdom, without patience, without sacrifice, and without God.

The supposition upon which I and others of my generation were brought up that in every life story the hero and the heroine ought always to marry and live happily ever after has led by an inevitable swing of the pendulum to a reaction of bitterness and disillusion, and the constant appeal to the divorce court as a remedy. The great natural gulfs that exist between any man and any woman, and between any one generation and the next, can no longer be hidden or ignored. They yawn out wide and threatening before the husbands and wives, the parents of children of our day, and menace the hope of a happy home. Our literature and art is largely concerned with emphasising their existence. The eternal triangle and the revolt of youth are the themes upon which they play with an almost nauseating persistence. The difficulties naturally inherent in the relationships of husbands to wives, and of parents to children have indeed always been felt, but seldom so widely and so keenly as they are felt to-day. This is largely due to the fact that the old bridges built by our fathers to span the gulf between husband and wife, parent and child, have broken down. The authority of the husband over the wife, and of the parent over the child, is much less absolute and a new freedom has arisen which immensely complicates both relationships.

God Save the King

The ideal of democracy has come to birth in the home as in the State. There has always been throughout history a curiously exact parallelism between the relationship of fathers to their families and of Kings and Rulers to their subjects. The home of the State have always acted and reacted the one upon the other. That is so in our day, and democracy with its ideals of freedom and equal comradeship has invaded both. Now, democracy is both difficult and dangerous. So difficult and dangerous as to drive even wise men to feelings of despair. It is difficult and dangerous because of the high demands it makes upon ordinary human nature. The success or failure of democracy, whether it be in the home or in the State, depends upon the character of the leaders. If parents are to be successful parents of comparatively free children, then they must be finer men and women, for their power will depend upon what they are in themselves. They will only be honoured because they are honourable, and obeyed because they are respected. If rulers are to be successful rulers of free people they will need to be finer men and women, for it is harder to inspire than to compel, more difficult to lead than to drive. Faced with awful responsibilities the rulers, whether it be of the little kingdoms or the large, may well be afraid and ask, " Who is sufficient for these things ? " But to be forewarned is to be forearmed, and it is only to cowards and weaklings that danger and difficulty are signals of despair. To the brave man or woman they are a challenge and a call.

This new age is a challenge and a call. A challenge and a call to which we can and will respond as we become filled with the spirit of Him who made a home at Nazareth and was crowned King of Kings with a crown of thorns and stoned on Calvary. The spirit of courage, service, and self-sacrifice is the spirit that alone can rule the homes and empires of the free. Every crown is a crown of thorns and every throne a calvary. I am the king of a tiny kingdom of three sons. I desire above all things on earth that they may grow up fair, and fine and free. Not seldom am I filled with fear of my responsibilities. And because of the knowledge which that fear brings, I pray—not as a form—but as an honest to God and goodness reality—I pray for the Father of that larger family of which my own is a loyal and a loving part—God save the King.

THE END

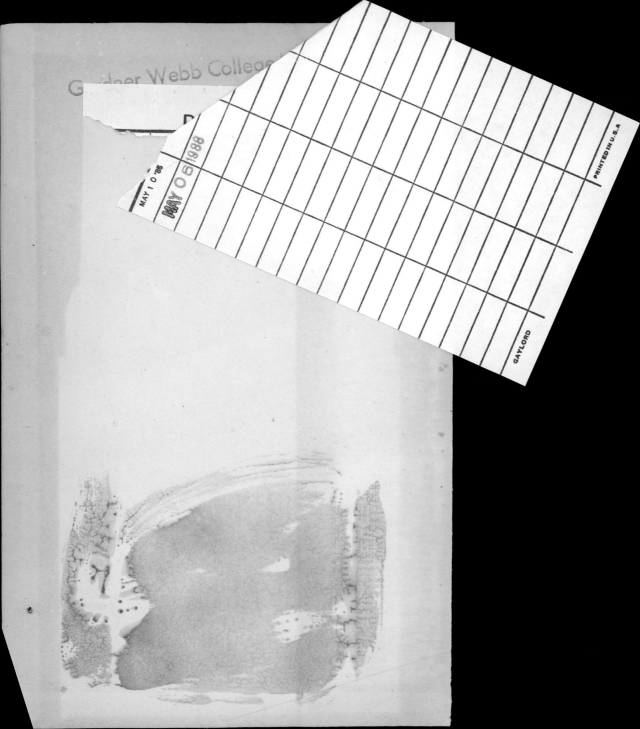